A Seaman's Anthology of Sea Stories

A Seaman's Anthology of Sea Stories

Compiled by

Desmond Fforde

Published by Accent Press Ltd – 2009

ISBN 9781906373986

Printed and bound in the UK

Cover Design by Red Dot Design

Introduction

I have placed these stories in chronological order, with a personal bias towards the Second World War. I hope that the reader will find that these stories are not as the usual run of anthologies.

'Hornblower and the Widow McCool' by C S Forester from *Hornblower and the Crisis*'. (Michael Joseph)
Hornblower is, of course, the best known fictional character in sea fiction. This short story is not well known, but illustrates the dilemmas which a young officer can be faced with on active service. I especially like the puzzle.

'Peter Simple' by Captain Marryat. (W. Nicholson & Sons, London) – date unknown.
Marryat was a midshipman under the famous Captain Cochrane, the model for many Napoleonic sea story heroes. This extract is particularly interesting to me because it is the only account I know of, of an extreme manoeuvre called 'club-hauling' – a desperate last resort to avoid the ship being driven ashore.

'Through the Gap' from *Down to the Sea* by 'Shalimar' (F C Hendry). (Blackwood & Sons, 1946)
Frank Hendry is without doubt my favourite sea-story writer. He had a distinguished career at sea in sailing and steam ships, and was a Rangoon pilot for some years. He then joined the Indian army and was awarded the MC for commanding a paddle steamer in the Tigris during the disastrous campaign in Mesopotamia (Iraq) in the First World War. He then,

in retirement, wrote many stories which were published by Blackwood's magazine in the 1940's and 1950's.

'On Camouflage, and Ships' Names' from *Merchantmen at Arms*, by Captain D Bone, (Chatto& Windus, 1919)
Captain Bone (later Sir David Bone) is well known for his book, *The Brassbounder*, taken from his apprenticeship in sail. He became Commodore master of the Anchor Line, and served throughout both world wars. His writing style is wonderfully archaic, and he is the only person who seems to have used the title 'Merchant's Service', a far more accurate forerunner to the later term, 'Merchant Navy'.

'I Was There' by Nicholas Monsarrat, from *The Ship That Died of Shame and Other Stories*. (Cassell, 1959)
A rather moving account of the Dunkirk evacuation from an imaginative point of view.

'Without Incident' by G. Drake, from *Touching the Adventures*. (G Harrap, 1953)
Geoffrey Drake was my first divisional officer when I, as a young cadet in HMS *Conway*, was training for the merchant navy. He was an unforgettable character and a seaman to his fingertips, as well as having many other artistic talents. His story well shows the sheer strain of operating in convoy; a strain unknown to modern seafarers.

'Quiet Holiday with a Genius' by Weston Martyr quoted in *More Joys of Life* by Uffa Fox. (Nautical Publishing Company [Harrap] 1972)

This story is a wonderful description of Uffa Fox at the height of his powers, when he was designing the Airborne Lifeboat, an extraordinary craft, one of which is on display at Newport, IOW. It is told in Weston Martyr's inimitable style.

'Send Down a Dove' by Charles MacHardy. (Collins, 1968)
This book is a real eye-opener for anyone who has read one of the conventional books on life in a submarine. Set at the close of WW2 in Europe, it is from the lower deck's point of view, and vividly portrays the squalor and cold of life aboard, and the heroic fatalism of the crew.

'Aircraft Carrier' by John Winton. (Michael Joseph, 1980)
A brilliant evocation of the life of a Fleet Air Arm pilot in the British Pacific Fleet in the closing stages of the war against Japan. This fleet was known as the 'forgotten fleet' as it did not have much publicity then, or since.

Contents

Hornblower and the Widow McCool

C S Forester

THE CHANNEL FLEET WAS taking shelter at last. The roaring westerly gales had worked up to such a pitch that timber and canvas and cordage could withstand them no longer, and nineteen ships of the line and seven frigates, with Admiral Lord Bridport flying his flag in HMS *Victory*, had momentarily abandoned that watch over Brest which they had maintained for six years. Now they were rounding Berry Head and dropping anchor in the shelter of Tor Bay. A landsman, with that wind shrieking round him, might be pardoned for wondering how much shelter was to be found there, but to the weary and weather-beaten crews who had spent so long tossing in the Biscay waves and clawing away from the rocky coast of Brittany, that foam-whitened anchorage was like paradise. Boats could even be sent in to Brixham and Torquay to return with letters and fresh water; in most of the ships, officers and men had gone for three months without either. Even on that winter day there was intense physical pleasure in opening the throat and pouring down it a draught of fresh clear water, so different from the stinking green liquid doled out under guard yesterday.

The junior lieutenant in HMS *Renown* was walking the deck muffled in his heavy pea jacket while his ship wallowed at her anchor. The piercing wind set his eyes watering, but he continually gazed through his telescope nevertheless; for, as signal lieutenant, he was responsible for the rapid reading and transmission of messages, and this was a likely moment for orders to be given regarding sick and stores, and for captains and admirals to start chattering together, for invitations to dinner to be passed back and forth, and even for news to be disseminated.

He watched a small boat claw its way towards the ship from the French prize the fleet had snapped up yesterday on its way up-Channel. Hart, master's mate, had been sent on board from the *Renown*, as prizemaster, miraculously making the perilous journey. Now here was Hart, with the prize safely anchored amid the fleet, returning on board to make some sort of report. That hardly seemed likely to be of interest to a signal lieutenant, but Hart appeared excited as he came on board, and hurried below with his news after reporting himself in the briefest terms to the officer of the watch. But only a very few minutes passed before the signal lieutenant found himself called upon to be most active.

I t was Captain Sawyer himself who came on deck, Hart following him, to supervise the transmission of the messages. 'Mr Hornblower!'

'Sir!'

'Kindly send this signal.'

It was for the admiral himself, from the captain; that part was easy; only two hoists were necessary to

2

say '*Renown* to Flag'. And there were other technical terms which could be quickly expressed – 'prize' and' French' and 'brig' – but there were names which would have to be spelled out letter for letter. 'Prize is French national brig *Espérance* having on board Barry McCool.'

'Mr James!' bellowed Hornblower. The signal midshipman was waiting at his elbow, but midshipmen should always be bellowed at, especially by a lieutenant with a very new commission.

Hornblower reeled off the numbers, and the signal went soaring up to the yardarm; the signal halyards vibrated wildly as the gale tore at the flags. Captain Sawyer waited on deck for the reply; this business must be important. Hornblower read the message again, for until that moment he had only studied it as something to be transmitted. But even on reading it he did not know why the message should be important. Until three months before, he had been a prisoner in Spanish hands for two weary years, and there were gaps in his knowledge of recent history. The name of Barry McCool meant nothing to him.

On the other hand, it seemed to mean a great deal to the admiral, for hardly had sufficient time elapsed for the message to be carried below to him than a question soared up to the *Victory*'s yardarm.

'Flag to *Renown*.' Hornblower read those flags as they broke and was instantly ready for the rest of the message. 'Is McCool alive?'

'Reply affirmative,' said Captain Sawyer.

And the affirmative had hardly been hoisted before the next signal was fluttering in the *Victory*.

'Have him on board at once. Court martial will

assemble.'

A court martial! Who on earth was this man McCool?

A deserter? The recapture of a mere deserter would not be a matter for the commander-in-chief. A traitor? Strange that a traitor should be court-martialled in the fleet. But there it was. A word from the captain sent Hart scurrying overside to bring this mysterious prisoner on board, while signal after signal went up from the *Victory* convening the court martial in the *Renown*.

Hornblower was kept busy enough reading the messages; he had only a glance to spare when Hart had his prisoner and his sea chest hoisted up over the port side. A youngish man, tall and slender, his hands were tied behind him – which was why he had to be hoisted in – and he was hatless, so that his long red hair streamed in the wind. He wore a blue uniform with red facings – a French infantry uniform, apparently. The name, the uniform, and the red hair combined to give Hornblower his first insight into the situation. McCool must be an Irishman. While Hornblower had been a prisoner in Ferrol, there had been, he knew, a bloody rebellion in Ireland. Irishmen who had escaped had taken service with France in large number. This must be one of them, but it hardly explained why the admiral should take it upon himself to try him instead of handing him over to the civil authorities.

Hornblower had to wait an hour for the explanation, until, at two bells in the next watch, dinner was served in the gun room.

'There'll be a pretty little ceremony tomorrow morning,' said Olive, the surgeon. He put his hand to

4

his neck in a gesture which Hornblower thought hideous.

'I hope the effect will be salutary,' said Roberts, the second lieutenant. The foot of the table, where he sat, was for the moment the head, because Buckland, the first lieutenant, was absent attending to the preparations for the court martial.

'But why should we hang him?' asked Hornblower.

Roberts rolled an eye on him.

'Deserter,' he said, and then went on. 'Of course, you're a newcomer. I entered him myself, into this very ship, in '98. Hart spotted him at once.'

'But I thought he was a rebel?'

'A rebel as well,' said Roberts. 'The quickest way out of Ireland – the only way, in fact – in '98 was to join the armed forces.'

'I see,' said Hornblower.

'We got a hundred hands that autumn,' said Smith, another lieutenant.

And no questions would be asked, thought Hornblower.

His country, fighting for her life, needed seamen as a drowning man needs air, and was prepared to make them out of any raw material that presented itself.

'McCool deserted one dark night when we were becalmed off the Penmarks,' explained Roberts. 'Got through a lower gunport with a grating to float him. We thought he was drowned until news came through from Paris that he was there, up to his old games. He boasted of what he'd done – that's how we knew him to be O'Shaughnessy, as he called himself when we had him.'

'Wolfe Tone had a French uniform,' said Smith.

'And they'd have strung him up if he hadn't cut his own throat first.'

'Uniform only aggravates the offence when he's a deserter,' said Roberts.

Hornblower had much to think about. First there was the nauseating thought that there would be an execution in the morning. Then there was this eternal Irish problem, about which the more he thought the more muddled he became. If just the bare facts were considered, there could be no problem. In the world at the moment, Ireland could choose only between the domination of England and the domination of France; no other possibility existed in a world at war. And it seemed unbelievable that anyone would wish to escape from English overlordship – absentee landlords and Catholic disabilities notwithstanding – in order to submit to the rapacity and cruelty and venality of the French republic. To risk one's life to effect such an exchange would be a most illogical thing to do, but logic, Hornblower concluded sadly, had no bearing upon patriotism, and the bare facts were the least considerable factors.

And in the same way the English methods were subject to criticism as well. There could be no doubt that the Irish people looked upon Wolfe Tone and Fitzgerald as martyrs, and would look upon McCool in the same light. There was nothing so effective as a few martyrdoms to ennoble and invigorate a cause.

The hanging of McCool would merely be adding fuel to the fire that England sought to extinguish. Two peoples actuated by the most urgent of motives – self-preservation and patriotism – were at grips in a struggle which could have no satisfactory ending for any lengthy time to come.

Buckland, the first lieutenant, came into the gun room with the preoccupied look commonly worn by first lieutenants with a weight of responsibility on their shoulders. He ran his glance over the assembled company, and all the junior officers, sensing that unpleasant duties were about to be allocated, did their unobtrusive best not to meet his eye. Inevitably it was the name of the most junior lieutenant which rose to Buckland's lips.

'Mr Hornblower,' he said.

'Sir!' replied Hornblower, doing his best now to keep resignation out of his voice.

'I am going to make you responsible for the prisoner.'

'Sir?' said Hornblower, with a different intonation.

'Hart will be giving evidence at the court martial,' explained Buckland – it was a vast condescension that he should deign to explain at all. 'The master-at-arms is a fool, you know. I want McCool brought up for trial safe and sound, and I want him kept safe and sound afterwards. I'm repeating the captain's own words, Mr Hornblower.'

'Aye, aye, sir,' said Hornblower, for there was nothing else to be said.

'No Wolfe Tone tricks with McCool,' said Smith. Wolfe Tone had cut his own throat the night before he was due to be hanged, and had died in agony a week later.

'Ask me for anything you may need, Mr Hornblower,' said Buckland.

'Aye, aye, sir.'

'Side boys!' suddenly roared a voice on deck

7

overhead, and Buckland hurried out; the approach of an officer of rank meant that the court martial was beginning to assemble.

Hornblower's chin was on his breast. It was a hard, unrelenting world, and he was an officer in the hardest and most unrelenting service in that world – a service in which a man could no more say 'I cannot' than he could say 'I dare not'.

'Bad luck, Horny,' said Smith, with surprising gentleness, and there were other murmurs of sympathy from round the table.

'Obey orders, young man,' said Roberts quietly. Hornblower rose from his chair. He could not trust himself to speak, so that it was with a hurried bow that he quitted the company at the table.

''E's 'ere, safe an' sound, Mr 'Ornblower,' said the master-at-arms, halting in the darkness of the lower 'tween decks.

A marine sentry at the door moved out of the way, and the master-at-arms shone the light of his candle lantern on a keyhole in the door and inserted the key.

'I put 'im in this empty storeroom, sir,' went on the master-at-arms. ''E's got two of my corporals along with 'im.'

The door opened, revealing the light of another candle lantern. The air inside the room was foul; McCool was sitting on a chest, while two of the ship's corporals sat on the deck with their backs to the bulkhead. The corporals rose at an officer's entrance, but even so, there was almost no room for the two newcomers. Hornblower cast a vigilant eye round the arrangements. There appeared to be no chance of escape or suicide. In the end, he steeled himself to meet

McCool's eyes.

'I have been put in charge of you,' he said.

'That is most gratifying to me, Mr – Mr –' said McCool, rising from the chest.

'Hornblower.'

'I am delighted to make your acquaintance, Mr Hornblower.'

McCool spoke in a cultured voice, with only enough of Ireland in it to betray his origin. He had tied back the red locks into a neat queue, and even in the faint candlelight his blue eyes gave strange reflections.

'Is there anything you need?' asked Hornblower.

'I could eat and I could drink,' replied McCool. 'Seeing that nothing has passed my lips since the *Espérance* was captured.'

That was yesterday. The man had had neither food nor water for more than twenty-four hours.

'I will see to it,' said Hornblower. 'Anything more?'

'A mattress – a cushion – something on which I can sit,' said McCool. He waved a hand towards his sea chest. 'I bear an honoured name, but I have no desire to bear it imprinted on my person.'

The sea chest was of a rich mahogany. The lid was a thick slab of wood whose surface had been chiselled down to leave his name – B. I. McCool – standing out in high relief.

'I'll send you in a mattress too,' said Hornblower. A lieutenant in uniform appeared at the door.

'I'm Payne, on the admiral's staff,' he explained to Hornblower. 'I have orders to search this man.'

'Certainly,' said Hornblower.

'You have my permission,' said McCool.

The master-at-arms and his assistants had to quit

the crowded little room to enable Payne to do his work, while Hornblower stood in the corner and watched. Payne was quick and efficient. He made McCool strip to the skin and examined his clothes with care – seams, linings, and buttons. He crumpled each portion carefully, with his ear to the material, apparently to hear if there were papers concealed inside. Then he knelt down to the chest; the key was already in the lock, and he swung it open. Uniforms, shirts, underclothing, gloves; each article was taken out, examined, and laid aside. There were two small portraits of children, to which Payne gave special attention without discovering anything.

'The things you are looking for,' said McCool, 'were all dropped overside before the prize crew could reach the *Espérance*. You'll find nothing to betray my fellow countrymen, and you may as well save yourself that trouble.'

'You can put your clothes on again,' said Payne curtly to McCool. He nodded to Hornblower and hurried out again.

'A man whose politeness is quite overwhelming,' said McCool, buttoning his breeches.

'I'll attend to your requests,' said Hornblower.

He paused only long enough to enjoin the strictest vigilance on the master-at-arms and the ship's corporals before hastening away to give orders for McCool to be given food and water, and he returned quickly. McCool drank his quart of water eagerly, and made an effort to eat the ship's biscuit and meat.

'No knife. No fork,' he commented.

'No,' replied Hornblower in a tone devoid of expression.

'I understand.'

It was strange to stand there gazing down at this man who was going to die tomorrow, biting not very efficiently at the lump of tough meat which he held to his teeth.

The bulkhead against which Hornblower leaned vibrated slightly, and the sound of a gun came faintly down to them. It was the signal that the court martial was about to open.

'Do we go?' asked Mc Cool.

'Yes.'

'Then I can leave this delicious food without any breach of good manners.'

Up the ladders to the main deck, two marines leading, McCool following them, Hornblower following him, and two ship's corporals bringing up the rear.

'I have frequently traversed these decks,' said McCool, looking round him, 'with less ceremonial.'

Hornblower was watching carefully lest he should break away and throw himself into the sea.

The court martial. Gold lace and curt efficient routine, as the *Renown* swung to her anchors and the timbers of the ship transmitted the sound of the rigging vibrating in the gale. Evidence of identification. Curt questions.

'Nothing I could say would be listened to amid these emblems of tyranny,' said McCool in reply to the President of the Court.

It needed no more than fifteen minutes to condemn a man to death: 'The sentence of this Court is that you, Barry Ignatius McCool, be hanged by the neck –'

The storeroom to which Hornblower escorted McCool back was now a condemned cell. A hurrying midshipman asked for Hornblower almost as soon as they arrived there.

'Captain's compliments, sir, and he'd like to speak to you.'

'Very good,' said Hornblower.

'The admiral's with him, sir,' added the midshipman in a burst of confidence.

Rear-Admiral the Honourable Sir William Cornwallis was indeed in the captain's cabin, along with Payne and Captain Sawyer. He started to go straight to the point the moment Hornblower had been presented to him.

'You're the officer charged with carrying out the execution?' he asked.

'Yes, sir.'

'Now look'ee here, young sir—'

Cornwallis was a popular admiral, strict but kindly, and of unflinching courage and towering professional ability. Under his nickname of 'Billy Blue' he was the hero of uncounted anecdotes and ballads. But having got so far in what he was intending to say, he betrayed a hesitation alien to his character. Hornblower waited for him to continue.

'Look'ee here,' said Cornwallis again. 'There's to be no speechifying when he's strung up.'

'No, sir?' said Hornblower.

'A quarter of the hands in this ship are Irish,' went on Cornwallis. 'I'd as lief have a light taken into the magazine as to have McCool make a speech to 'em.'

'I understand, sir,' said Hornblower.

But there was a ghastly routine about executions. From time immemorial the condemned man had been allowed to address his last words to the onlookers.

'String him up,' said Cornwallis, 'and that'll show 'em what to expect if they run off. But once let him open his mouth — that fellow has the gift of the gab, and we'll have this crew unsettled for the next six months.'

'Yes, sir.'

'So see to it, young sir. Fill him full o' rum, maybe. But let him speak at your peril.'

'Aye, aye, sir.'

Payne followed Hornblower out of the cabin when he was dismissed.

'You might stuff his mouth with oakum,' he suggested. 'With his hands tied he could not get it out.'

'Yes,' said Hornblower, his blood running cold.

'I've found a priest for him,' went on Payne, 'but he's Irish too. We can't rely on him to tell McCool to keep his mouth shut.'

'Yes,' said Hornblower.

'McCool's devilish cunning. No doubt he'd throw everything overboard before they capture him.'

'What was he intending to do?' asked Hornblower.

'Land in Ireland and stir up fresh trouble. Lucky we caught him. Lucky for that matter, we could charge him with desertion and make a quick business of it.'

'Yes,' said Hornblower.

'Don't rely on making him drunk,' said Payne, 'although that was Billy Blue's advice. Drunk or sober, these Irishmen can always talk. I've given you the best hint.'

'Yes,' said Hornblower, concealing a shudder.

He went back into the condemned cell like a man condemned himself. McCool was sitting on the straw mattress Hornblower had had sent in, and the two

13

ship's corporals still had him under their observation.

'Here comes Jack Ketch,' said McCool with a smile that almost escaped appearing forced.

Hornblower plunged into the matter in hand; he could see no tactful way of approach.

'Tomorrow –' he said.

'Yes, tomorrow?'

'Tomorrow you are to make no speeches,' he said.

'None? No farewell to my countrymen?'

'No.'

'You are robbing a condemned man of his last privilege.'

'I have my orders,' said Hornblower.

'And you propose to enforce them?'

'Yes.'

'May I ask how?'

'I can stop your mouth with tow,' said Hornblower brutally.

McCool looked at the pale, strained face. 'You do not appear to me to be the ideal executioner,' said McCool, and then a new idea seemed to strike him. 'Supposing I were to save you that trouble?'

'How?'

'I could give you my parole to say nothing.' Hornblower tried to conceal his doubts as to whether he could trust a fanatic about to die.

'Oh, you wouldn't have to trust my bare word,' said McCool bitterly. 'We can strike a bargain, if you will. You need not carry out your half unless I have already carried out mine.'

'A bargain?'

'Yes. Allow me to write to my widow. Promise me to send her the letter and my sea chest here – you can

14

see it is of sentimental value – and I, on my side, promise to say no word from the time of leaving this place here until – until –' Even McCool faltered at that point. 'Is that explicit enough?'

'Well –' said Hornblower.

'You can read the letter,' added McCool. 'You saw that other gentleman search my chest. Even though you send these things to Dublin, you can be sure that they contain nothing of what you would call treason.'

'I'll read the letter before I agree,' said Hornblower. It seemed a way out of a horrible situation. There would be small trouble about finding a coaster destined for Dublin; for a few shillings he could send letter and chest there.

'I'll send you in pen and ink and paper,' said Hornblower.

It was time to make the other hideous preparations.

To have a whip rove at the portside fore yardarm, and to see that the line ran easily through the block. To weight the line and mark a ring with chalk on the gangway where the end rested. To see that the noose ran smooth. To arrange with Buckland for ten men to be detailed to pull when the time came. Hornblower went through it all like a man in a nightmare.

Back in the condemned cell, McCool was pale and wakeful, but he could still force a smile.

'You can see that I had trouble wooing the muse,' he said.

At his feet lay a couple of sheets of paper, and Hornblower, glancing at them, could see that they were covered with what looked like attempts at writing poetry. The erasures and alterations were numerous.

'But here is my fair copy,' said McCool, handing

15

over another sheet.

'My darling wife,' the letter began. 'It is hard to find words to say farewell to my very dearest –'

It was not easy for Hornblower to force himself to read that letter. It was as if he had to peer through a mist to make out the words. But they were only the words of a man writing to his beloved, whom he would never see again. That at least was plain. He compelled himself to read through the affectionate sentences. At the end it said: 'I append a poor poem by which in the years to come you may remember me, my dearest love. And now goodbye, until we shall be together in heaven. Your husband, faithful unto death, Barry Ignatius McCool.'

Then came the poem.

> 'Ye heavenly powers! Stand by me when I die!
> The bee ascends before my rolling eye.
> Life still goes on within the heartless town.
> Dark forces claim my soul. So strike 'em down.
> The sea will rise, the sea will fall. So turn
> Full circle. Turn again. And then will burn
> The lambent flames while hell will lift its head.
> So pray for me while I am numbered with the dead.'

Hornblower read through the turgid lines and puzzled over their obscure imagery. But he wondered if he would be able to write a single line that would make sense if he knew he was going to die in a few hours.

'The superscription is on the other side,' said McCool, and Hornblower turned the sheet over. The letter was addressed to the Widow McCool, in some street in Dublin. 'Will you accept my word now?' asked McCool.

'Yes,' said Hornblower.

16

The horrible thing was done in the grey hours of the morning.

'Hands to witness punishment.'

The pipes twittered and the hands assembled· in the waist, facing forward. The marines stood in lines across the deck. There were masses and masses of white faces, which Hornblower saw when he brought McCool up from below. There was a murmur when McCool appeared. Around the ship lay boats from all the rest of the fleet, filled with men – men sent to witness the punishment, but ready also to storm the ship should the crew stir. The chalk ring on the gangway, and McCool standing in it. The signal gun; the rush of feet as the ten hands heaved away on the line. And McCool died, as he had promised, without saying a word.

The body hung at the yardarm, and as the ship rolled in the swell that came round Berry Head, so the body swung and dangled, doomed to hang there until nightfall, while Hornblower, sick and pale, began to seek out a coaster which planned to call at Dublin from Brixham, so that he could fulfil his half of the bargain. But he could not fulfil it immediately; nor did the dead body hang there for its allotted time. The wind was backing northerly and was showing signs of moderating. A westerly gale would keep the French fleet shut up in Brest; a northerly one might well bring them out, and the Channel fleet must hurry to its post again. Signals flew from the flagships.

'Hands to the capstan!' bellowed the bosun's mates in twenty-four ships. 'Hands make sail!'

With double-reefed topsails set, the ships of the Channel fleet formed up and began their long slant down-Channel. In the *Renown* it had been, 'Mr

Hornblower, see that *that* is disposed of.' While the hands laboured at the capstan the corpse was lowered from the yardarm and sewn into a weighted bit of sailcloth. Clear of Berry Head it was cast overside without ceremony or prayer. McCool had died a felon's death and must be given a felon's burial. And, close-hauled, the big ships clawed their way back to their posts amid the rocks and currents of the Brittany coast.

And on board the *Renown* there was one unhappy lieutenant, at least, plagued by dreadful memories.

In the tiny cabin which he shared with Smith there was something that kept Hornblower continually reminded of that morning: the mahogany chest with the name 'B. I. McCool' in high relief on the lid. And in Hornblower's letter case lay that last letter and the rambling, delirious poem. Hornblower could send neither on to the widow until the *Renown* should return again to an English harbour, and he was irked that he had not yet fulfilled his half of the bargain. The sight of the chest under his cot jarred on his nerves; its presence in their little cabin irritated Smith.

Hornblower could not rid his memory of McCool; nor, beating about in a ship of the line on the dreary work of blockade, was there anything to distract him from his obsession. Spring was approaching and the weather was moderating. So that when he opened his leather case and found that letter staring at him again, he felt undiminished that revulsion of spirit. He turned the sheet over; in the half dark of the little cabin he could hardly read the gentle words of farewell. He knew that strange poem almost by heart, and he peered at it again, sacrilege though it seemed to try to analyse the thoughts of the brave and frightened man who had

18

written it during his final agony of spirit. 'The bee ascends before my rolling eye.' What could possibly be the feeling that inspired that strange imagery? 'Turn full circle. Turn again.' Why should the heavenly powers do that?

A startling thought suddenly began to wake to life in Hornblower's mind. The letter, with its tender phrasing, had been written without correction or erasure. But this poem; Hornblower remembered the discarded sheets covered with scribbling. It had been written with care and attention. A madman, a man distraught with trouble, might produce a meaningless poem with such prolonged effort, but then he would not have written that letter. Perhaps –

Hornblower sat up straight instead of lounging back on his cot. 'So strike 'em down.' There was no apparent reason why McCool should have written ''em' instead of 'them'. Hornblower mouthed the words. To say 'them' did not mar either euphony or rhythm. There might be a code. But then why the chest? Why had McCool asked for the chest to be forwarded with its uninteresting contents of clothing? There were two portraits of children; they could easily have been made into a package. The chest with its solid slabs of mahogany and its raised name was a handsome piece of furniture, but it was all very puzzling.

With the letter still in his hand, he got down from the cot and dragged out the chest. B. I. McCool. Barry Ignatius McCool. Payne had gone carefully through the contents of the chest. Hornblower unlocked it and glanced inside again; he could see nothing meriting particular attention, and he closed the lid again and turned the key. B. I. McCool. A secret compartment! In a fever, Hornblower opened the chest again, flung out the contents and examined sides and bottom. It called for only the briefest examination to assure him that there was no room there for anything other than a microscopic secret compartment. The lid was thick and heavy, but he could see nothing suspicious about it. He closed it again and fiddled with the raised letters, without result.

He had actually decided to replace the contents when a fresh thought occurred to him. 'The bee ascends!' Feverishly Hornblower took hold of the 'B' on the lid. He pushed it, tried to turn it. 'The bee ascends!' He put thumb and finger into the two hollows in the loops of the 'B', took a firm grip and pulled upward. He was about to give up when the letter yielded a little, rising up out of the lid half an inch. Hornblower opened the box again, and could see nothing different. Fool that he was! 'Before my rolling eye.' Thumb and forefinger on the 'I'. First this way, then that way — and it turned!

Still no apparent further result. Hornblower looked at the poem again. 'Life still goes on within the heartless town.' He could make nothing of that. 'Dark forces claim my soul.' No. Of course! 'Strike 'em down.' That ''em'. Hornblower put his hand on the 'M' of 'McCool' and pressed vigorously. It sank down into the lid. 'The sea will rise, the sea will fall.' Under firm pressure the first 'C' slid upward, the second 'C' slid downward. 'Turn full circle. Turn again.' Round went one 'O', and then round went the other in the opposite direction. There was only the 'L' now. Hornblower glanced at the poem. 'Hell will lift its head.' He guessed it at once; he took hold of the top of the 'L' and pulled;

the letter rose out of the lid as though hinged along the bottom, and at the same moment there was a loud decisive click inside the lid. Nothing else was apparent, and Hornblower gingerly took hold of the lid and lifted it. Only half of it came up; the lower half stayed where it was, and in the oblong hollow between there lay a mass of papers, neatly packaged.

The first package was a surprise. Hornblower, peeping into it, saw that it was a great wad of five-pound notes — a very large sum of money. A second package was similar. Ample money here to finance the opening moves of a new rebellion. The first thing he saw inside the next package was a list of names, with brief explanations written beside each. Hornblower did not have to read very far before he knew that this package contained the information necessary to start the rebellion. In the last package was a draft proclamation ready for printing. 'Irishmen!' it began.

Hornblower took his seat on the cot again and tried to think, swaying with the motion of the ship. There was money that would make him rich for life. There was information which, if given to the government, would clutter every gallows in Ireland. Struck by a sudden thought, he put everything back into the chest and closed the lid.

For the moment it was a pleasant distraction, saving him from serious thought, to study the ingenious mechanism of the secret lock. Unless each operation was gone through in turn, nothing happened. The 'I' would not turn unless the 'B' was first pulled out, and it was most improbable that a casual investigator would pull at that 'B' with the necessary force. It was most unlikely that anyone without a clue would ever discover how to open the lid, and the joint in the wood was marvellously well concealed. It occurred to Hornblower that when he should announce his discovery matters would go badly with Payne, who had been charged with searching McCool's effects. Payne would be the laughing-stock of the fleet, a man both damned and condemned.

Hornblower thrust the chest back under the cot and, secure now against any unexpected entrance by Smith, went on to try to think about his discovery. That letter of McCool's had told the truth. 'Faithful unto death.' McCool's last thought had been for the cause in which he died. If the wind in Tor Bay had stayed westerly another few hours, that chest might have made its way to Dublin. On the other hand, now there would be commendation for him, praise, official notice – all very necessary to a junior lieutenant with no interests behind him to gain him his promotion to captain. And the hangman would have more work to do in Ireland. Hornblower remembered how McCool had died, and felt fresh nausea at the thought. Ireland was quiet now. And the victories of St Vincent and the Nile and Camperdown had put an end to the imminent danger which England had gone through. England could afford to be merciful. He could afford to be merciful. And the money?

Later on, when Hornblower thought about this incident in his past life; he cynically decided that he resisted temptation because bank notes are tricky things, numbered and easy to trace, and the ones in the chest might even have been forgeries manufactured by the French government. But Hornblower misinterpreted his own motives, possibly in self-defence, because they were so vague and so muddled that he was ashamed of them.

He wanted to forget about McCool. He wanted to think of the whole incident as closed.

There were many hours to come of pacing the deck before he reached his decision, and there were several sleepless nights. But Hornblower made up his mind in the end, and made his preparations thoughtfully, and when the time came he acted with decision. It was a quiet evening when he had the first watch; darkness had closed in on the Bay of Biscay, and the *Renown*, under easy sail, was loitering along over the black water with her consorts just in sight. Smith was at cards with the purser and the surgeon in the gun room. A word from Hornblower sent the two stupidest men of the watch down below to his cabin to carry up the sea chest, which he had laboriously covered with canvas in preparation for this night. It was heavy; for buried among the clothing inside were two twenty-four-pound shot. They left it in the scuppers at Hornblower's order. And then, when at four bells it was time for the *Renown* to tack, he was able, with one tremendous heave, to throw the thing overboard. The splash went unnoticed as the *Renown* tacked.

There was still that letter. It lay in Hornblower's writing case to trouble him when he saw it. Those tender sentences, that affectionate farewell; it seemed a shame that McCool's widow should not have the privilege of seeing them and treasuring them. But – but- when the *Renown* lay in the Hamoaze, completing for the West . Indies, Hornblower found himself sitting at dinner next to Payne. It took a little while to work the conversation around in the right direction.

'By the way,' said Hornblower with elaborate casualness, 'did Mc Cool leave a widow?'

'A widow? No. Before he left Paris he was involved in a notorious scandal with La Gitanita, the dancer. But no widow.'

'Oh,' said Hornblower.

That letter, then, was as good a literary exercise as the poem had been. Hornblower realized that the arrival of a chest and a letter addressed to the Widow McCool at that particular house in Dublin would have received the attention it deserved from the people who lived there. It was a little irritating that he had given so much thought to the widow, but now the letter could follow the chest overside. And Payne would not be made the laughing-stock of the fleet.

Peter Simple

Captain Marryat

WE CONTINUED OUR CRUISE along the coast, until we had run down into the Bay of Arcason, where we captured two or three vessels, and obliged many more to run on shore. And here we had an instance showing how very important it is that a captain of a man-of-war should be a good sailor, and have his ship in such discipline as to be strictly obeyed by his ship's company. I heard the officers unanimously assert, after the danger was over, that nothing but the presence of mind which was shown by Captain Savage could have saved the ship and her crew. We had chased a convoy of vessels to the bottom of the bay: the wind was very fresh when we hauled off, after running them on shore; and the surf on the beach even at that time was so great, that they were certain to go to pieces before they could be got afloat again. We were obliged to double-reef the topsails as soon as we hauled to the wind, and the weather looked very threatening. In an hour afterwards, the whole sky was covered with one black cloud, which sank so low as nearly to touch our mast-heads, and a tremendous sea, which appeared to have risen up almost by magic, rolled in upon us, setting the vessel on a dead lee shore. As the night closed in, it blew a dreadful gale, and the ship was nearly buried with the press of canvas which she was obliged to carry: for had we sea-room, we should have been lying-to under storm staysails; but we were. forced to carry on at all risks, that we might claw off shore. The sea broke over as we lay in the trough, deluging us with water from the forecastle, aft, to the binnacles; and very often, as the ship descended with a plunge, it was with such force that I really thought she would divide in half with the violence of the shock. Double breechings were rove on the guns, and they were further secured with tackles; and strong cleats nailed behind the trunnions; for we heeled over so much when we lurched, that the guns were wholly supported by the breechings and tackles, and had one of them broken loose, it must have burst right through the lee side of the ship, and she must have foundered. The captain, first lieutenant, and most of the officers remained on deck during the whole of the night; and really, what with the howling of the wind, the violence of the rain, the washing of the water about the decks, the working of the chain-pumps, and the creaking and groaning of the timbers, I thought that we must inevitably have been lost; and I said my prayers at least a dozen times during the night, for I felt it impossible to go to bed. I had often wished, out of curiosity, that I might be in a gale of wind; but I little thought it was to have been a scene of this description, or anything half so dreadful. What made it more appalling was, that we were on a lee shore, and the consultations of the captain and officers, and the eagerness with which they looked out for daylight, told us that we had other dangers to encounter besides the storm. At last the morning broke, and the look-out man upon the gangway called out, "Land on the lee beam!" I perceived the master dash his feet against the hammock-rails, as if with vexation, and walk away without saying a word, and looking very grave.

"Up there, Mr. Wilson," said the captain to the second lieutenant, "and see how far the land trends forward, and whether you can distinguish the point." The second lieutenant· went up the main-rigging, and pointed with his hand to about two points before the beam.

"Do you see two hillocks inland?"

"Yes, sir," replied the second lieutenant.

"Then it is so," observed the Captain to the master, "and if we weather it we shall have more sea-room. Keep her full, and let her go through the water; do you hear, quarter-master?"

"Ay, ay, sir."

"Thus, and no nearer, my man. Ease her with a spoke or two when she sends; but be careful, or she'll take the wheel out of your hands."

It really was a very awful sight. When the ship was in the trough of the sea, you could distinguish nothing but a waste of tumultuous water; but when she was borne up on the summit of the enormous waves, you then looked down, as it were upon a low, sandy coast, close to you, and covered with foam and breakers. "She behaves nobly," observed the captain, stepping aft to the binnacle, and looking at the compass; "if the wind does not baffle us, we shall weather." The captain had scarcely time to make the observation, when the sails shivered and flapped like thunder. "Up with the helm; what are you about, quarter-master?"

"The wind has headed us, sir," replied the quartermaster, coolly.

The captain and master remained at the binnacle watching the compass; and when the sails were again full, she had broken off two points, and the point of land was only a little on the lee bow.

"We must wear her round, Mr. Falcon. Hands, wear ship – ready, oh, ready."

"She has come up again," cried the master, who was at the binnacle.

"Hold fast there a minute. How's her head now?"

"N.N.E., as she was before she broke off, sir."

"Pipe belay," said the captain. "Falcon," continued he, "if she breaks off again we may have no room to wear; indeed there is so little room now, that I must run the risk. Which cable was ranged last night – the best bower?"

"Yes, sir."

"Jump down, then, and see it double-bitted and stoppered at thirty fathoms. See it well done – our lives may depend upon it."

The ship continued to hold her course good; and we were within half a mile of the point, and fully expected to weather it, when again the wet and heavy sails flapped in the wind, and the ship broke off two points as before. The officers and seamen were aghast, for the ship's head was right on to the breakers. "Luff now, all you can, quarter-master," cried the captain. "Send the men aft directly. My lads, there is no time for words – I am going to club-haul the ship, for there is no room to wear. The only chance you have of safety is to be cool, watch my eye, and execute my orders with precision. Away to your stations for tacking ship. Hands by the best bower anchor. Mr. Wilson, attend below with the carpenter and his mates, ready to cut away the cable at the moment that I give the order. Silence, there, fore and aft. Quarter-master, keep her full again for stays. Mind you ease the helm down when I tell you." About a minute passed before the captain gave any further orders. The ship had closed – to within a quarter-mile – of the beach, and the waves curled and topped around us, bearing us down upon the shore, which presented one continued surface of foam, extending to within half a cable's length of our position. The captain waved his hand in silence to the quarter-master at the wheel, and the helm was put down. The ship turned slowly to the wind, pitching and chopping as the sails were spilling. When she had lost her way, the captain gave the order, "Let go the anchor. We will haul all at once, Mr. Falcon," said the captain. Not a word was spoken; the men went to the fore brace, which had not been manned, most of them knew, although I did not, that if the ship's head did not go round the other way, we should be on shore, and among the breakers in half a minute. I thought at the time that the captain had said that he would haul all the yards at once, there appeared to be doubt or dissent on the countenance of Mr. Falcon; and I was afterwards told that he had not agreed with the captain; but he was too good an officer, and knew that there was no time for discussion, to make any remark; and the event proved that the captain was right. At last the ship was head to wind, and the captain gave the signal. The yards flew round with such a creaking noise that I thought the masts had gone over the side; and the next moment the wind had caught the sails; and the ship, which for a moment or two had been on an even keel, careened over to her gunnel with its force. The captain, who stood upon the weather-hammock rails, holding by the main-rigging, ordered the helm amidships, looked full at the sails, and then at the cable, which grew broad upon the weather bow, and held the ship from nearing the shore. At last he cried, "Cut away the cable!" A few strokes of the axes were heard, and then the cable flew out, of the hawse-hole in a blaze of fire, from the violence of the friction, and disappeared under a huge wave, which struck us on the chess-tree, and deluged us with water fore and aft. But we were now on the other tack, and the ship regained her way, and we had evidently increased our distance from the land.

"My lads," said the captain, to the ship's company, "you have behaved well, and I thank you; but I must tell you honestly that we have more difficulties to get through. We have to weather a point of the bay on this tack. Mr. Falcon, splice the main-brace, and call the watch. How's her head, quarter-master?"

"S.W. by S. Southerly, sir."

"Very well; let her go through the water;" and the captain, beckoning to the master to follow him, went down into the cabin. As our immediate danger was over, I went down into the berth to see if I could get anything for breakfast, where I found O'Brien and two or three more.

"By the powers, it was as nate a thing as ever I saw done," observed O'Brien: "the slightest mistake as to time or management, and at this moment the flatfish would have been dubbing at our ugly carcases. Peter, you're not fond of flatfish are you, my boy? We may thank Heaven and the captain, I can tell you that, my lads: but now, where's the chart, Robinson? Hand me down the parallel rules and compasses, Peter; they are in the corner of the shelf. Here we are now, a devilish sight too near this infernal point. Who knows how her head is?"

"I do, O'Brien: I heard the quarter-master tell the captain S.W. by S. Southerly."

"Let me see," continued O'Brien, "variation 2¼ – lee way-rather too large an allowance of that, I'm afraid; but, however, we'll give her 2½ points; the Diomede would blush to make any more, under any circumstances. Here – the compass – now we'll see;" and O'Brien advanced the parallel rule from the compass to the spot where the ship was placed on the chart. "Bother! you see it's as much as she'll do to weather the other point now, on this tack, and that's what the captain meant when he told us we had more difficulty. I could have taken my Bible oath that we were clear of everything, if the wind held."

"See what the distance is, O'Brien," said Robinson.

It was measured, and proved to be thirteen miles. "Only thirteen miles; and if we do weather, we shall do very well, for the bay is deep beyond. It's a rocky point, you see, just by way of variety. Well, my lads, I've a piece of comfort for you, anyhow. It's not long that you'll be kept in suspense, for by one o'clock this day, you'll either be congratulating each other upon your good luck, or you'll be past praying for. Come, put up the chart, for I hate to look at melancholy prospects; and, steward, see what you can find in the way of comfort." Some bread and cheese, with the remains of yesterday's boiled pork, were put on the table, with a bottle of rum, procured at the time they "spliced the mainbrace"; but we were all too anxious to eat much; and one by one returned on deck to see how the weather was, and if the wind at all favoured us. On deck the superior officers were in conversation with the captain, who had expressed the same fear that O'Brien had in our berth. The men, who knew what they had to expect, were assembled in knots, looking very grave, but at the same time not wanting in confidence. They knew that they could trust to the captain, as far as skill or courage could avail them; and sailors are too sanguine to despair, even at the last moment. As for myself, I felt such admiration for the captain, after what I had witnessed that morning, that, whenever the idea came over me, that in all probability I should be lost in a few hours, I could not help acknowledging how much more serious it was that such a man should be lost to his country. I do not intend to say that it consoled me; but it certainly made me still more regret the chances with which we were threatened.

Before twelve o'clock the rocky point which we so much dreaded was in sight, broad on the lee-bow; and if the low sandy coast appeared terrible, how much more did this, even at a distance. The captain eyed it for some minutes in silence, as if in calculation.

"Mr. Falcon," said he, at last, "we must put the mainsail on her."

"She never can bear it, sir."

"She must bear it," was the reply. "Send the men aft to the mainsheet. See that careful men attend the buntlines."

The mainsail was set, and the effect of it upon the

ship was tremendous. She careened over so that her lee channels were under the water; and when pressed by a sea, the lee-side of the quarter deck and gangway were afloat.

She now reminded me of a goaded and fiery horse, mad with the stimulus applied, not rising as before, but forcing herself through whole seas, and dividing the waves, which poured in one continual torrent from the forecastle down upon the decks below. Four men were secured to the wheel – the sailors were obliged to cling, to prevent being washed a way – the ropes were thrown in confusion to lee-ward, the shot rolled out of the lockers, and every eye was fixed aloft, watching the masts which were expected every moment to go over the side. A heavy sea struck us on the broadside, and it was some moments before the ship I appeared to recover herself; she reeled, trembled, and stopped her way, as if it had stupefied her. The first lieutenant looked at the captain, as if to say, "This will not do." "It is our only chance," answered the captain to the appeal. That the ship went faster through the water, and held a better wind, was certain; but just before we arrived at the point the gale increased in force. "If anything starts, we are lost, sir," observed the first lieutenant again.

"I am perfectly aware of it," replied the captain, in a calm tone; "but, as I said before, and you must now be aware, it is our only chance. The consequence of any carelessness or neglect in the fitting and securing of the rigging will be felt now; and this danger, if we escape it, ought to remind us how much we have to answer for if we neglect our duty. The lives of a whole ship's company may be sacrificed by the neglect or incompetence of an officer when in harbour. I will pay you the compliment, Falcon, to say, that I feel convinced that the masts of the ship are as secure as knowledge and attention can make them."

The first lieutenant thanked the captain for his good opinion, and hoped it would not be the last compliment which he paid him.

"I hope not, too; but a few minutes will decide the point."

The ship was now within two cable's lengths of the rocky point. Some few of the men I observed to clasp their hands, but most of them were silently taking off their jackets and kicking off their shoes, that they might not lose a chance of escape, provided the ship struck.

"'Twill be touch and go, indeed, Falcon," observed the captain (for I had clung to the belaying-pins, close to him for the last half-hour that the mainsail had been set). "Come aft; you and I must take the helm. We shall want nerve there, and only there, now."

The captain and first lieutenant went aft, and took the forespokes of the wheel, and O'Brien, at a sign made by the captain, laid hold of the spokes behind him. An old quarter-master kept his station at the fourth. The roaring of the seas on the rocks, with the howling of the wind, were dreadful; but the sight was more dreadful than the noise. For a few moments I shut my eyes but anxiety forced me to open them again. As near as I could judge, we were not twenty yards from the rocks at the time that the ship passed abreast of them. We were in the midst of the foam, which boiled around us; and as the ship was driven nearer to them, and careened with the wave, I thought that our main yard-arm would have touched the rock; and at this moment a gust of wind, came on which laid the ship on her beam-ends, and checked her progress through the water, while the accumulated noise was deafening. A few moments more the ship dragged on, another wave dashed over her and spent itself upon the rocks, while the spray was dashed back from them, and returned upon the decks. The main rock was within ten yards of her counter, when another gust of wind laid us on our beam-ends, the foresail and mainsail split and were blown clean out of the bolt-ropes – the ship righted, trembled fore and aft. I looked astern: the rocks were to windward on our quarter, and we were safe. I thought at the time that the ship, relieved of her courses, and again lifting over the waves, was not a bad similitude of the relief felt by us all at that moment; and, like her, we trembled as we panted with the sudden reaction, and felt the removal of the intense anxiety which oppressed our breasts.

The captain resigned the helm, and walked aft to look at the point, which was now broad on the weather quarter. In a minute or two he desired Mr. Falcon to get new sails up and bend them, and then went below to his cabin. I am sure it was to thank God for our deliverance: I did most fervently, not only then, but when I went to my hammock at night. We were now comparatively safe – in a few hours completely so; for strange to say, immediately after we had weathered the rocks, the gale abated, and before morning we had a reef out of the topsails. It was my afternoon watch, and perceiving Mr. Chucks on the forecastle, I went forward to him, and asked him what he thought of it.

"Thought of it, sir!" replied he; "why, I always

think bad of it when the elements won't allow my whistle to be heard; and I consider it hardly fair play. I never care if we are left to our own exertions; but how is it possible for a ship's company to do their best when they cannot hear the boatswain's pipe? However, God be thanked, nevertheless, and make better Christians of us all! As for that carpenter, he is mad. Just before we weathered the point, he told me that it was just the same 27,600 and odd years ago. I do believe that on his death-bed (and he was not far from a very hard one yesterday), he will tell us how he died so many thousand years ago, of the same complaint. And that gunner of ours is a fool. Would you believe it, Mr. Simple, he went crying about the decks, 'O my poor guns, what will become of them if they break loose?' He appeared to consider it of no consequence if the ship and ship's company were all lost provided that his guns were safely landed on the beach. 'Mr. Dispart,' said I, at last, 'allow me to observe, in the most delicate way in the world, that you're a d-d old fool.' You see, Mr. Simple, it's the duty of an officer to generalize, and be attentive to parts only in consideration of the safety of the whole. I look after my anchors and cables as I do after the rigging; not that I care for any of them in particular, but because the safety of a ship depends, upon her being well found. I might just as well cry because we sacrificed an anchor and cable yesterday morning, to save the ship from going on shore."

"Very true, Mr. Chucks," replied I.

"Private feelings," continued he, "must always be sacrificed for the public service. As you know, the lower deck was full of water, and all our cabins and chests were afloat; but I did not think then about my shirts:

and look at them now, all blowing out in the forerigging, without a particle of starch left in the collars or the frills. I shall not be able to appear as an officer ought to do for the whole of the cruise."

As he said this, the cooper, going forward, passed by him, and jostled him in passing. "Beg pardon, sir," said the man, "but the ship lurched."

"The ship lurched, did it?" replied the boatswain, who, I am afraid, was not in the best of humours about his wardrobe, "And pray, Mr. Cooper, why has Heaven granted you two legs with joints at the knees, except to enable you to counteract the horizontal deviation? Do you suppose they were meant for nothing but to work round a cask with? Hark, sir! did you take me for a post to scrub your pig's hide against? Allow me just to observe, Mr. Cooper – just to insinuate – that when you pass an officer it is your duty to keep at a respectful distance, and not to soil his clothes with your rusty iron jacket. Do you comprehend me, sir; or will this make you recollect in future?" The rattan was raised, and descended in a shower of blows, until the cooper made his escape into the head. "There, take that, you contaminating, stave-dubbing, gimlet-carrying, quintessence of a bung-hole! I beg your pardon, Mr. Simple, for interrupting the conversation; but when duty calls we must obey."

"Very true, Mr. Chucks. It's now striking seven bells, and I must call the master – so good-by."

Through the Gap

'Shalimar' (F C Hendry)

ONLY THIRTY YEARS AGO speed in sailing ships still counted for much; even at the end of the nineties the season's wool from the Antipodes was being raced home by clippers – often oversparred and exciting to handle – which were manned by crews large enough to enable a press of sail to be carried with the probability that it could be reduced before damage to spars and canvas resulted. Then any ship that made a passage of a hundred days from Australia to London was looked on as a crawler. Today sailing vessels still come from Australia, but instead of wool they bring wheat. In their own deliberate, poverty-stricken way they race, but for them a hundred days is a brilliant passage. They are generally old British ships – built for carrying rather than for speed – and their rigging plans have in many cases been cut down. They are undermanned, and their small crews consist mainly of boys, so that work aboard them is desperately hard, and they cannot hang on to their canvas when the wind freshens. They are mostly owned by Finns, but there is an occasional Swede. All honour to them! But for their hardihood, square sail, with all it stands for in the maritime history of the world, would have vanished from the face of the waters; and when the square-rigged ship does finally vanish, the world will lose a brave and a fine art matured slowly and painfully in the course of many years.

In November 1895, the beautiful, full-rigged, iron clipper ship *Revoan* lay alongside Circular Quay in Sydney. She looked rather lonely. A month before she had not wanted for company, for a line of her tall sisters, whose spars and rigging had formed a vast network against the sky, nestled against the quay. Then one after the other, in charge of fussy little tugs, they had departed; clipper after clipper, having received her quota of wool, put out to sea. Brave days! Brave ships! All had been designed for speed, and they had to produce it; all were built on fine lines and rigged with heavy spars; amongst them were some of the loveliest ships that ever sailed the ocean.

Still the *Revoan* lingered on, graceful and still, like a great bird longing to spread its wings. Truth to tell, she was rather in disgrace; she no longer received the first of the wool clip, but that was really no fault of hers. For years she had raced with the best of them and always held her own; then her passages began to lengthen, and everyone in the business knew the reason – the white-haired veteran who commanded her since she left the stocks had lost his nerve. Her passages lengthened still more until they became abnormal. Her exasperated owners knew the reason too, but hesitated to dispense with the services of an old servant and friend. Then, just as they had decided they could put up with him no longer, he resigned – to their great relief.

A young captain, who had only been in command for about eighteen months, took over the *Revoan* and made a good outward passage with her. He was keen, energetic and capable, and speed was his god. To achieve it at sea he had spared no pains over her trim while she was being loaded. Now he was itching to get away, determined that his famous clipper would, by the time she returned to Sydney, be worthy of the honour of racing again with the first of the season's wool.

At last it was the *Revoan*'s turn to be hauled away from the quay by a fussy little tug. Outside the Heads she picked up a strong westerly wind; lying over heavily, and with every sail she carried set and drawing, she romped away across the Tasman Sea. Five days out she passed Campbell Island far south of New Zealand and shaped a more easterly course for Cape Horn. Hard-pressed by her thrusting, impatient, young captain, she flew before the fresh straight-lined gale and the great seas that raced up behind her, and on the twenty-fifth day out from Sydney she was right off the pitch of the Horn, but far to the south of it. There she met a barque outward bound to Valparaiso and signalled 'All well.'

All was not really well, however, aboard the *Revoan*. Generally speaking, she was quite a happy ship, but almost from the beginning of the outward voyage friction had existed among her officers. To begin with, the mate was twice the age of the captain, and he had been passed over so often for promotion that he was soured. When Captain Byrne was appointed to command the *Revoan*, Mr Jenkins, who had been mate of her for seven voyages, almost resigned. Only one thing kept him from doing so: he loved the beautiful clipper as a mother loves her child. For he had tended her with affectionate care aloft and below; he knew every detail in her from truck to keelson. Indeed, as the custodian of her internal economy he was uncomfortably efficient. No one could tell him a thing he did not know about that ship's outfit from a washer in the fresh-water pump to the sheave-pin in the main-truck, as both the captain and the second mate had found to their discomfiture. On several uncomfortable occasions he had contradicted them, bluntly but rightly, and caused them both to blush. No cleaner or better kept vessel ever lay in Sydney Harbour, and for this Captain Byrne got much credit which really belonged to Mr Jenkins, as the captain freely admitted. There was rarely any friction in port, but it broke out again almost as soon as the *Revoan* went to sea.

The friction was not due to difference in ages nor to incompatibility of temper. The explanation of it was even simpler than that. Captain Byrne, anxious to take every ounce out of a fair wind, was all for carrying as much sail as the ship could stagger under – as has been said, speed was his god. The second mate – a youngster not long out of his apprenticeship and with little experience to guide him – would crack on until all was blue. But a precipitous leaning deck, a broad sheet of hissing white foam to leeward and the inclination of tall masts and cracking yards overburdened with sails, seemed to be too much for the old mate's nerves; A conversation which took place in a bar-parlour in Sydney between Mr Jenkins and a crony who was mate of another ship throws some light on the former's opinion of the young second mate, and also indirectly of the captain, although he was never mentioned. Mr Jenkins was much too loyal a member of the old school to discuss his 'old man' with anybody.

"She'll be run under some day," he said gloomily, "and the best of it is that young squirt thinks he's a hell of a sailor. Mark my words, if he doesn't run her under he'll have the sticks out of her. When you hear she has been dismasted — well, it won't have happened in my watch."

"Any fool can carry sail on a ship," quoth the crony, wagging his head solemnly.

"Ay, but it takes a seaman like the last captain to know when to take it in," Mr Jenkins replied.

Using that old adage to quell any misgiving he might have about his nerves, the mate doggedly went his way. Time after time the captain had gone up on the poop during Mr Jenkins' watch on deck at night to find the clipper, instead of running along at a good twelve knots, was snugged down so that she was only doing a bare ten. The mate's excessive caution probably accounted for his lack of promotion. A thoroughly competent seaman, if a rather timid navigator, he could have taken some apple-bowed, comfortable old tub safely round the seas without the loss of a rope-yarn; but he would have been of little use in command of a ship the chief aim of which was to make quick passages from port to port.

On one occasion Captain Byrne, sick to death of his subordinate's timidity, went below at midnight, leaving definite orders that sail was not to be taken in. The result was that Mr Jenkins turned mulish; for once his obstinacy overcame his great love for the *Revoan*, and the captain, thrown off the settee in his stateroom onto the floor by a frightful lurch, had gone on deck to find a black squall howling overhead, the ship almost on her beam-ends and the mate hanging on to the weather rail with the evident intention of doing nothing even if she capsized.

That experiment was evidently too dangerous to be repeated, and a complete deadlock between captain and mate as to the carrying of sail ensued, for it was obvious the captain could not be on deck the whole time. It was a galling situation for an eager shipmaster, and it caused considerable dissatisfaction among the crew also; for when the wind was strong and favourable, about half the time the men of the port watch – which the mate led – were on deck would be spent in taking in sail, while half the starboard watch's spell would be spent in setting it again. When it is said that, in addition to his other characteristics, Mr Jenkins was a confirmed and croaking pessimist, it will be understood he was rather an uncomfortable companion for a young skipper making his second voyage in command.

Now that the *Revoan* had reached the Horn and was just about to turn north into the Atlantic, the weather moderated, although a heavy swell still rolled up astern. With the breeze four points on the port quarter and all plain sail, except the crossjack, set, she sailed steadily eastward.

At four o'clock on the morning after the outward-bounder was sighted, Mr Jenkins left his room and went on the poop. He approached the second mate with a monosyllabic grunt, growled something to the assembled hands that was meant to be, "Relieve the wheel and look-out," and took over charge of the deck. At exactly five minutes past four he knocked at the door of Captain Byrne's stateroom. The captain, who, as was his habit in those stormy latitudes, was lying on his settee fully dressed with the exception of his boots, shouted, "Come in!"

Mr Jenkins opened the stateroom door, walked across to the swing lamp which was burning dimly and turned it up. Clad in gleaming, long, black oilskin coat, sou'-wester, and thigh gum-boots, he looked rather incongruous in the cosy room with its carpeted floor and dainty chintz curtains.

"Sir," he said, "I would like you to come on deck at once. It's so thick with snow that I can't see my hand in front of my face. I think we should bring her up to the wind and head-reach until it clears."

"What is she doing, Mr Jenkins?"

"About nine knots when they hove the log at eight bells, sir," the mate replied.

"It seems a great pity to stop her, Mr Jenkins. We are well to the s'uth'ard, and it's highly improbable anything will be in the way."

"What about an outward-bounder standing close-hauled, across our bows? I can't see the loom of our own sidelights from the main-deck, let alone those of another ship."

"Daylight will be coming in soon," the captain suggested hopefully. "Couldn't we keep her going till then and sound the fog-horn frequently?"

"That's the worst of it, sir; one of those damned Dutchmen in the starboard watch has burst the fog-horn up," the mate replied gloomily. "Daylight won't make much difference, anyhow; the snowflakes are too heavy."

The fog-horn – a semi-mechanical gadget – had never been a very efficient instrument. It required an expert to produce the proper blasts on it – three of them when the ship was running free, two when on the port tack and one when on the starboard – but when they were produced they could at least attract an answering wail from any vessel in the immediate vicinity which would thus indicate her whereabouts. Even this slight aid to safe navigation was now denied the *Revoan*. Captain Byrne sighed and sat up on his settee.

"All right!" he said with resignation, "I'll be up in a minute."

Dressing did not take him as long as that. He had merely to pull on his sea-boots, don his oilskin coat and his sou'-wester, and he was ready. When he emerged from the companionway on to the poop he gasped because of the cold wind that caught his lungs like a knife-stab. His sea-booted feet, instead of treading firmly on the deck planks, slithered in a soft carpet of snow; also he seemed to be enclosed on all sides by an impenetrable veil. The mate's statement that he could not see his hand in front of his face had been literally true; not only the officer and the look-out, but every man of the watch on deck was completely blindfolded. Captain Byrne, five seconds after he left the companionway, lost his bearings; he staggered about until he reached the teakwood rail that ran round the poop, then, clinging to it, he felt his way aft to the binnacle, in which there was a light. He bumped into the mate, who was standing beside it, and who looked like a snowman.

"How long has it been as thick as this?" he demanded. "Since about two o'clock, sir; so the second mate told me," Mr Jenkins replied readily.

He felt an inward glow of satisfaction; without having said anything spiteful he got his own back on the young squirt that time, had shown up his careless and reckless ways.

"H'm!" said the captain, after a pause for thought. "Let the yards go for'a'd on the backstays and I'll bring her up to the wind."

Shouting, "Lee fore brace" as he went, the mate stamped along the poop on his way down to the main-deck. For once in a way at that dreary hour the men obeyed him cheerfully. Not long out of their warm bunks, they had been hanging miserably around the break of the poop, shaking the snow off themselves, stamping on the deck and flapping their hands across their chests in a vain endeavour to restore circulation to their fingers. The exercise of hauling the yards forward – indeed, any exercise – would be welcome. Captain Byrne, standing at the break of the poop, wished he could join the invisible little mob, for he suddenly realised that he had never felt colder in his life. He was shivering, his feet were numb, even his very breath as he exhaled seemed to freeze on his lips.

From forward he could hear ropes – found by instinct, in that almost solid darkness, with seamanlike precision – being thrown off belaying-pins, blocks whirring as the braces ran through their sheaves, parrals creaking as the great yards swung forward and the musical shouts of the men as they hauled. Then above all other sounds came the stentorian bellow of the mate.

"Well the fore-yards! Belay!"

"*Belay!*"

From out of the darkness to leeward, away clear of the ship altogether, the order was loudly and distinctly repeated. At the weird sound incredulous men looked fearfully at each other; then their eyes strained to pierce the opaque wall of snow through which the mysterious voice had sounded so clearly. There could be nothing on the rolling sea away out there! Nothing human! Was it supernatural, a warning of impending doom? The more superstitious thought, and shivered anew. The uneasy silence was broken by the voice of the captain; yes, it was his voice, though for the moment they hardly recognised it, for it was husky with horror.

"Down helm! Hard down!" they heard him shout. "Let the after-yards stand. All hands on deck!"

Terror-stricken, the men of the watch below swarmed out on deck asking vain, breathless questions which no one could answer. The *Revoan*'s head began to swing up to the wind; very slowly it swung because of the pressure of the heavy swell that was running against her. To help the rudder the yards on the mizzen were braced forward and the mainsail hauled up. The ship came up more rapidly then; the sails on the main shivered as the wind caught their leaches, slatted, and crashed for an instant as the ship's head swung toward the wind, then remained firm, pressed hard against the mast, for the wind was now in front of them. Now she was broadside on to the swell and wallowing in it, and the helm was steadied. With the sails on the fore and mizzen full of wind and exerting their power to drive her forward, and the sails on the main aback and retarding her, she lay almost hove-to, moving ahead at the rate of about one knot. Mr Jenkins, his job finished, went up the poop ladder and approached the captain, whom he could see dimly.

"What's the matter, sir?" he faltered.

"Matter! *Ice*! Close to! The *echo*! My God! Why wasn't I called before?"

Daylight began to appear, and in spite of the mate's pessimistic forecast it did make some difference. Its first effect was to separate individual snowflakes from the dense veil that had previously enveloped the ship. Presently men could see the heaving sea alongside; it looked cold and grey; its surface was effervescent with dissolving snowflakes. The whole of the snow-encrusted shape that was the *Revoan* became dimly visible, but a few yards beyond her no man could see. Softly and silently the flakes drifted, presenting an impenetrable barrier to vision.

The captain stood beside the binnacle, sniffing and listening, since sight was denied him. Suddenly he realised the mate was nearby – a stocky figure leaning on the wheel-box. A wave of gratitude, which swamped all previous irritation, a feeling which was akin to affection for his elderly subordinate, came to Captain Byrne. He shuddered to think what would have happened had the second mate remained in charge of the deck for another hour. or the mate had not been so prompt in insisting sturdily on his presence on deck: a wild, last-moment shout from the man on the look-out on the forecastle-head, a crash, a break-up, confusion, a short struggle in the icy water – then the end! Bless Mr Jenkins' grizzled old head!

Beyond the creaking of a yard aloft, or the slat of a

sail, there was now almost a complete silence; even the splashing of the waves against the weather side of the hull seemed to be strangely noiseless. The hands – too worried now to notice the cold – lined the starboard rail, straining to get a glimpse of what lay to leeward. At last they got it; a ghostly luminous strip of white lay all along the lee beam – the ice blink. The ship, drifting dead to leeward with every heave of the swell, was closing on it, and suddenly the roar of surf breaking on the bases of icebergs was plain to every ear.

At that moment the snowflakes became smaller and more intermittent, and two minutes afterwards they ceased falling. The sky to windward cleared, and the weather horizon showed up in an unbroken line. Then a gleaming white object appeared on the weather bow, showing vividly against the dark water in which it was sitting and the grey sky. It was their first glimpse of the ice, but much more was to follow, for, as the curtain of snow dissolved, a magnificent but terrifying spectacle revealed itself. From broad off on the weather bow, right ahead, along the lee beam, and even out on the weather quarter, there stretched a continuous rampart of ice – flat-topped like a plateau, and some hundreds of feet high. Its intense whiteness dazzled the eyes. It was shaped like a gigantic letter L, and how long the legs of the L were no man could guess, for the outer ends of them were lost to vision in the dim horizon. It was one of the largest ice islands ever known to have broken away from its parent, the Great Ice Barrier, and reach so far north. That year several vessels bound round Cape Horn went missing and no man of their crews ever returned to tell of their fate. How many of them did that wandering ice island destroy?

With sinking heart but impassive face, Captain Byrne stood on the poop and studied the situation. It looked hopeless. In the darkness the *Revoan* had sailed right into the angle formed by the legs of the L, and was now less than a mile from the heel, and standing diagonally across it from one leg to the other. The southerly leg was less than half a mile away, under her stern, so she must have been close alongside it when she was brought up into the wind. Only dead to windward was the horizon clear, and escape that way was, for a sailing vessel, obviously impossible. The captain gazed at the ice barrier. How high waves rise in the open sea is still an unsolved question; that they rise far higher when they meet opposition such as cliffs and icebergs is certain; they seemed to be running up the face of that rampart of ice to a height of something like a hundred feet, and it would take them a very short time to pound a vessel to pieces.

It seemed impossible to save the ship; she was drifting rapidly straight to destruction, and would be no better off on the other tack. Already the captain was thinking of the boats – but what a ghastly prospect! The *Revoan*, forging slowly ahead, was slightly altering the shapes of the contours of the ice, and suddenly a slit seemed to open up in it, two points abaft the lee beam. The captain thought he could see through the slit to open water beyond, and he stared at it as if fascinated. It grew rather wider, and he dashed to the companionway for his telescope. Still the rift in the ice seemed to grow. For some reason – perhaps the iceberg had split and the halves were drifting apart – *the legs of the L were not joined together!*

The captain ran to the binnacle and took a bearing

of the rift and the wind; the rift was dead to leeward; it looked terribly narrow, but it seemed to offer the only avenue of escape.

"Hard up the helm! Lay the yards dead square!" he shouted confidently.

Mr Jenkins gave the initial order in his fog-horn voice.

"Square the main and cro'-jick yards!" he roared. Instinctively, without waiting for a reason for the order, he went down on to the main-deck to supervise the operation. The sheaves in the brace-blocks seemed reluctant to move, and it was some little time before the great yards began to swing. When they did, the *Revoan's* head, under the influence of her helm and the altered trim of the sails, swung slowly away before the wind and sea until it pointed straight at the rift; and it was not until the mate had completed operations by trimming the fore-yards also that he looked ahead and realised what was happening. When he did he waddled aft as fast as his rather corpulent figure and the state of the snow-clad deck would allow, climbed the poop ladder, and addressed himself to his commander.

"Captain Byrne, are you mad, sir?" he cried hoarsely. "She'll never go through there."

"Mr Jenkins," the captain began deliberately, "if she doesn't she'll never go through anything else in this world, nor will a single soul aboard of her. My God! man," he continued fiercely, "aren't you sailor enough to see it's our only chance? Haul the foresail up so that we can see the ship's head beneath it, and send Munro to the wheel."

Munro – a lanky, casual youth – was the senior apprentice.

In his reaction against modern officers, Mr Jenkins – who had come in through the hawse-pipe and did not approve of premium apprentices – took rather a delight in harassing this budding one. Almost every day he rubbed it into Munro that, like Reuben Ranzo, he was more of a tailor than a sailor; and only that morning he had proposed a new profession for the erring youth.

"*You* an officer in square sail, you lazy hoodlum!" he said with scorn. "Damn me, it's a barber's clerk you ought to be, and it's all you're fit for."

The prospective 'barber's clerk' was undoubtedly lazy, but in spite of his laziness – indeed, perhaps because of it – he was the finest helmsman in the ship. Not for him the wheel spinning hard up and hard down! Once he assumed control he used the minimum amount of helm; and if the ship did wander half a point off her course and had to be brought back to it, he seemed to have an uncanny instinct as to the exact moment the wheel had to be moved to meet her returning swing. While the hands rushed forward to man clew-garnets and bunt-lines with which to haul the foresail up, Munro strolled along the lee side of the poop, crossed over to windward, and relieved the wheel just in time. The man who was at it lost his nerve when the ice came ahead, and the captain had knocked him away from it and seized it himself. The toe of a boot restored him to his senses and propelled him forward to where there was work afoot.

"Do you see that channel between those two icebergs?" the captain asked the apprentice.

"Yes, sir!"

"Well, steer straight for the centre of it."

"Straight for the centre of it, sir!" Munro repeated.

Captain Byrne walked forward a few paces, then returned to the wheel.

"Munro!" he said in a voice that would have frightened the life out of anyone else on board, "steer as you never steered before! God! boy, keep her right in the middle if you want to see Scotland again."

Munro's dreamy eye was fixed on the rift ahead; he nonchalantly twirled the wheel a couple of spokes.

"Ay, ay, sir," he replied.

Among the group of men down on the main-deck – a few lethargic, some anxious, one or two terror-stricken – was a Newfoundlander who had been in .the sealing business and knew something about ice. He looked ahead toward the rift, then shrugged his shoulders pessimistically.

"Guess the old man's clean forgotten we've got yards sticking out both sides," he drawled.

Apart from that remark there was a death-like silence on board the *Revoan* as the snow-shrouded clipper, looking as white and ghostly as the icebergs themselves, glided toward the streak of water that lay between them. Pitching with the swell, but going along noiselessly at a speed of about six knots with the wind dead behind her, she crept nearer and nearer to the mysterious floating islands, and the spell of their eerie loneliness fell on all hands. They were near enough now to notice details of formation and colour. Just where the running swell worked up into long rollers that curled over and rushed with a thunderous roar up the face of the ice-cliffs, the sea was turned a light green by reflected light from hundreds of feet of submerged ice. Where the rollers washed up their faces the bergs glistened dark green; above the highest levels of the waves the creviced and corniced precipices were weathered white, and freshly fallen snow lay deep on their ledges.

Across the mouth of the rift there stretched a ridge of water; it was so much beneath the level of the rollers breaking on the ice that it looked like a depression between them, but it was higher than the swell which caused it by banking up in an endeavour to press through the opening. Beyond the foaming ridge the narrow lane of water resembled a mountain pass. Was there room for the ship to get through? The strait only looked about thirty yards wide, and the *Revoan*'s main-yard measured ninety feet from yard-arm to yard-arm. On the poop and main-deck there was strained suspense.

The jib-boom reached the entrance and the bow began to climb the hill of water which seemed to block it. Up the ship went till she was perched, shuddering, on the crest, while the tortured surf churned all round her; then down with a sickening plunge to find the black water of the gap almost smooth. Recovering herself she moved smoothly forward. For a time, with the exception of Munro, coolly turning the wheel a spoke or two at a time and steering beautifully, not a man moved a muscle; then simultaneously necks were craned and eyes stared aloft to see if the yard-arms were going to clear. To the anxious watchers it appeared to be touch and go. To what height the icebergs on both sides towered precipitously no one knew; certainly they loomed high above the main-truck, and that was one hundred and sixty feet from the deck. Men shuddered with a sense of the awe-inspiring lifelessness of that dark and awful gap.

God! What a strange, gloomy, sombre hell it looked! And cold! Cold as the grave! On both sides the walls of ice seemed to be so near men felt they could have touched them with a boat-hook. They were flying past with surprising rapidity too, as if some invisible tide-rip was helping the ship through. The *Revoan* was still sailing at the rate of about six knots, but the closeness of the ice gave the impression that she was going much faster, and this illusion of speed added to the nervous strain.

Soon the whole length of the ship was in the channel, and still she glided on unscathed. Captain Byrne stood beside the wheel staring fixedly at the clear water ahead; his gaze had been steadily averted from the yard-arms as if he did not dare to look at them; not once did he speak to or interfere with Munro, upon whom alone the immediate safety of the ship depended. The mate was at the fore-end of the poop, gripping the teakwood rail with an intensity that had turned his knuckles white. The young second mate, almost unnerved, had turned his back to everything; his shoulders were hunched, and he was looking down at the poop deck planks. Along the main-deck the hands stood in scared, silent groups; not one of them even ventured to whisper. The black cook had come out of the galley; his great eyes rolled in his black face, his white teeth gleamed, his surprised demeanour seemed to express the thought, "Golly, what are we doing in here?" The youngest apprentice – a lad of sixteen – saw him and suddenly burst into shrieks of hysterical laughter. The shrieks echoed back weirdly from the walls of ice; it was ghastly!

On the clipper stole. She seemed to have passed the narrowest part of the channel; yes, it was undoubtedly widening; she would soon be clear. Just then, however, Captain Byrne saw to his astonishment that, instead of being a couple of hundred yards broad as he had imagined them to be when he surveyed them from the other side, the islands of ice still stretched about a mile ahead of the ship. The channel between them, however, splayed out into a bay which would be at least a quarter of a mile across at its outer extremity, so that was all right. The *Revoan* debouched from the defile into the ever-widening waters of the bay, and the strain on all hands eased. From dry throats down on the main-deck there came a faint cackle which was meant for a cheer.

Then the cheer died away promptly, strangled at birth, for at that moment the sails flapped noisily once or twice, then hung limply up and down the masts. The eyes of all hands turned aft to look for a reason, and they were not long in finding it. The gap which they had just threaded had almost closed up behind them, and blocked the following wind which was blowing as through a funnel. Under the influence of some mysterious ocean current, operating on their bases hundreds of fathoms below the surface, the great islands of ice were coming together again. What an escape!

Men blanched, trembled, and broke into profuse perspiration in spite of the cold.

For a time the *Revoan* carried her way toward the open sea; good luck to the naval architect who designed her to ghost along with a minimum of wind – sometimes even with the flap of her sails. True, she could not get very far, but she was clear of the narrow gap, and with the ice a hundred and fifty yards away on both sides there was no immediate danger. Again the men began to chatter amongst themselves, and to discuss the fate they had been so lucky to escape. They were premature, they had not escaped yet; though nearly through to the other side of the L they were by no means clear, and the captain was the first to discover the real gravity of their situation.

Gazing aft he noticed that pivoting backward on the inside point of the heel of the L, where the gap was naturally narrowest, the flat-topped, clean cut, inner extremities of the bergs were moving toward each other. The long legs of the L were bending outward in an endeavour to straighten that letter out, with the result that their feet were coming together with the intention of joining. The mile-long, sheer coast-lines of the bay, quite three hundred feet high, resembled the blades of a great shears, with the fork of the shears at the now almost closed rift and the points at the two outer capes they could see ahead. And the blades of the shears were steadily closing. Soon there would be no bay! A more unnerving thought could hardly come into the mind of man!

The thought certainly shook Captain Byrne considerably, but it did not unnerve him. He looked over the side; bubbles of foam were floating aft – the *Revoan* was still moving ahead. From astern there came a great crunching noise; the floating masses had met and outlying pinnacles and crags were splitting and grinding each other to pieces. The unyielding bases, under the inexorable pressure from below, locked together and held; the blades of the shears began to close more rapidly. The *Revoan* could not carry her way very much longer, for not a breath of wind reached her sails. Clearly there was not a single minute to spare.

"Mr Jenkins, swing out the two after boats, put enough men in them to double-bank the oars, and tow her out clear," the captain ordered confidently.

The operation seemed feasible enough, especially if the boats could get ahead and commence towing before the way was off the ship. There would be no initial inertia to be overcome, and the *Revoan* had such fine lines that it took little force to keep her moving ahead; the sea under the lee of the icebergs was as calm as a sheltered mill pond. Instantly there was a rush of eager men toward the skids where the boats rested nine feet above the main-deck. With frantic hands they cut the lashings that secured the boats, tore off the boat-covers, and hooked on the davit-tackles. The sun came out through the clouds and flooded the white cliffs that lay around with a dazzling light.

Then an unfortunate hitch occurred round the boats; the sheaves in the davit-tackle blocks were frozen up and refused to move. Sobbing and gasping with the intensity of their efforts, the hands hauled like demons on the falls, which hung in bights, but the rock-like ropes would only render through the blocks an inch at a time so long as the sheaves refused to work. In his impatience Captain Byrne beat a tattoo with his right foot on the poop deck.

"Get boiling water from the galley," Mr Jenkins roared from his central position on top of the half-deck.

Men hurried along the main-deck to carry out the order, but the delay had been fatal, for by this time the *Revoan* was almost stopped. She had not sufficient steerage-way left; her head was falling off lazily to starboard.

"Steering, Munro?" the captain asked anxiously.

"No, sir! The helm's hard over!"

It was hopeless now to try to tow the ship clear, for she would have to be straightened up so that her head would point seaward first; and while it might be possible to drag three thousand five hundred tons straight ahead, they could never twist it. Still the precipitous white blades of the shears were inexorably closing; by this time, grinding and clashing against each other with irresistible power, they had met a hundred yards nearer.

"Get those boats into the water for God's sake!" the captain shouted. "Steward, get some provisions into them quick! All hands abandon ship!"

The dullest-witted man aboard could see the danger now, and the feverish activity round the boats was redoubled, although one or two of the more terror-stricken – such as the man who had just left the wheel and one of his countrymen – seemed too paralysed to work. At the instigation of Mr Jenkins, the second mate, who was very useful with his fists, soon knocked the paralysis out of them. As the boiling water was poured on the blocks the hands again hauled like madmen on the davit-tackle falls. The sheaves began to work grudgingly and the falls came tight; slowly and reluctantly, an inch at a time, the boats parted from the skids. The outside chocks were frozen to the skids and had to be knocked away with a maul. Everything seemed to hamper the frantic race against time. Captain Byrne – after a despairing look round at the gigantic ice-trap relentlessly closing its jaws, the calm black water between the bergs in which the clipper floated motionless and helpless, and the sails hanging limply up and down, the masts – rushed down to his stateroom to collect the ship's papers.

As he unscrewed the chronometer box a shaft of sunlight came through a glass port and shone on a picture hanging on the bulkhead. It was a picture that was very precious to him; indeed, many things in that room were precious to him, but there was neither time to remove them nor room in the boats for them. Still, it was hard to part with his household gods; that room was the only home he had, and the ship's cat – it came aboard as a kitten in London – purring at the foot of his bunk made the room look more homely still.

While the captain worked rapidly his thoughts were bitter, though the bitterness was slightly sweetened by the knowledge that he could hardly blame himself; his luck was just completely out. Last night's setting sun had looked on as lovely a picture as the ocean could show – a wool-clipper, with every stitch of canvas on her, pressing homeward; tonight it would look for that clipper in vain. She would be a mutilated, distorted thing – embedded in an overwhelming mass of ice; her bulwarks would be smashed, her hull plates cracked, her decks stove in and her yards telescoped. In that ice she would remain, imprisoned and unseen, until at some distant date it had floated far enough north to become dissolved; then she would finally drop clear and sink to the ocean bed, the glowing future he had dreamed for her irretrievably ruined. And the men of her crew! The best fortune they could expect was to be adrift in open boats exposed to the cruel capricious winds, high seas and biting cold of the great lonely southern ocean; and from what the captain had seen when he left the deck they would indeed be fortunate if they got that far. If the ship had no future, *theirs* was immediately intense and momentous.

The last thought quickened his movements. He grabbed the cat by the scruff of the neck, then, with the ship's papers in his pocket and sextant and chronometer under his arms, he hurried toward the companionway. In the cabin the steward was hastily packing tins into a box, and the cook was staggering out through the door in the break of the poop with a sack of cabin biscuits on his back. Bidding them hurry, Captain Byrne dashed up the stairs. As he emerged on to the poop he noticed that there was a comparative silence on the main-deck; the shouting and tumult of men hauling on ropes had ceased; the hands were manning the davit-guys, or swarming up on to the skids to swing out the boats which now hung from the davit-heads. A rather plaintive voice spoke from aft.

"She's steering again, sir," said Munro.

Absolutely astounded, the captain stared aloft to find out how this miracle had happened, and saw that the main royal – the highest sail of all – was bulging out nobly and tugging at its containing sheets. He looked over the side; specks of foam were again floating aft. He looked ahead; the jib-boom was slowly swinging to port; before long the *Revoan* would once more be heading straight toward the open sea. Still greater luck to the naval architect who had designed a ship with lines so perfect that even a little royal, full of wind, was sufficient to send her forging ahead with steerage-way! The captain walked to the break of the poop, then back to the companionway, craned his neck and again looked aloft; the mizzen royal and half the main upper topgallant-sail had also filled with wind, whiffs of which were blowing downward from the top of the ice behind them.

"Hold on everything," he shouted joyfully, and dropped the disgusted cat in the snow.

The ring of confidence in his voice, almost as much as the order, caused the mates and the men to pause hopefully and look around them. So intent had all hands been on getting out the boats — the only instruments, so far as they knew, that could save them from being crushed to death — they had not noticed anything else. Now they also craned their necks and gazed aloft, and, as they stood in suspense, one or two of them commenced to whistle softly — the time-honoured expedient used by windjammer sailors for bringing more wind. More wind came, in ever-freshening puffs. The strip of open water behind her widened, and the farther the ship got away from the lee of the bergs the more merrily the breeze blew.

The *Revoan* picked up her way smartly and was gaining on the converging ice, which rapidly altered its bearing as she slipped past it. The sails on the mizzen were all drawing now. On she swept; the wake, clear-cut in the calm water, began to foam, and soon she shot in triumph between the two capes marking the exit from the bay. As she reached the open water beyond, Captain Byrne looked round anxiously. In addition to the barrier to the west through which the ship had just passed there were icebergs of all shapes and sizes stretching away to the north and south as far as the eye could reach.

"All the blasted ice in the southern ocean seems to

be gathered round here," he growled.

So far as he could see, however, there was open water to the eastward, and after all that was the direction in which he wished to proceed.

"Slip up on to the fore topgallant yard, mister," he said to the second mate, "and let me know if there is any ice to the north-east."

The hands began to lower the boats into their positions on the skids, and to secure them again; there would, please Providence, be no use for them now. It was a pleasing thought, but it did not prevent Mr Jenkins – in spite of his relief – from staring ruefully at the hacked lashings and the torn boat-covers. Such extravagant waste grieved him beyond measure. A hail came from the fore topgallant yard.

"On deck!"

"Hullo!"

"All clear to the nor'-east, sir!"

"Good!" the captain commented. "Mr Jenkins, get every stitch of canvas on her and let's get away out of this."

The foresail, mainsail and crossjack were set and the yards trimmed. The breeze freshened; on her new course the *Revoan* had it about two points abaft the beam, and she lay over to it until the water gurgled in through her lee scupper-holes. It was now a day for glorious exhilarating sailing, a day of vivid. blues and whites – blue sky, blue sea; dazzling white icebergs astern and to windward, white horses racing on the crests of the waves, white foam creaming past in broad bands. The keen wind whistled through the rigging and caused each billowing sail to tug lustily at its sheets and fastenings. The watch below was dismissed and, thoroughly well pleased with life, the captain was about to leave the poop when the mate approached.

"Captain Byrne," he said rather shamefacedly, "I wish I had some of your nerve. My God! sir, I could do with it."

"Mr Jenkins," the captain replied frankly, "I wish I had some of your cautious commonsense; that's a commodity I could certainly do with. Now, look here! I'm just going below to have a cup of coffee, and I'm going to add a good dash of brandy to it for once in a way. She's quite safe now, so the second mate can look after her for a bit. (A subtle one, that.) Will you join me?"

Mr Jenkins looked away toward the distant horizon.

When he turned to his captain again his weather-beaten face was slightly distorted, his lips twitched, and there was a suspicion of moisture in his usually keen grey eyes. He put out his hand and Captain Byrne grasped it.

"Come away below," the younger man said kindly.

When, a quarter of an hour later, the mate returned to the poop and relieved the second mate, he was more gracious to that boyish officer than he had been on any occasion since the ship left Sydney; after all, the young squirt had proved himself a capable man-driver and a loyal colleague when they were striving desperately to get the boats clear of the skids. Mr Jenkins went down on the main-deck and walked slowly round it inspecting the gear with an eye that missed nothing. He turned the hands to, to clear the snow off the decks, for at no time during the hours of daylight could he bear to see a man idle; then he noticed Munro furtively emerging from the half-deck where, on being relieved from the wheel and seeing no signs of the mate, he had gone for a surreptitious smoke and yarn with the apprentices of the watch below.

"What the hell were you doing in there?" the mate growled.

"Having a drink of water, sir," Munro lied glibly.

"A drink of water!" Mr Jenkins snorted.

He still felt a warm inward glow from the drink he had imbibed, and he was perfectly certain no one would want to drink water on a morning like that.

"Look here!" he continued, "there's one thing about you — you can steer. I'll give you full marks for that; and when everything else fails perhaps you'll get a job as quartermaster in a steamboat. (It is impossible to convey the disdain which Mr Jenkins contrived to put into the word 'steamboat'.) But don't get swollen-headed about it. The next time I catch you in that house during your watch on deck I'll fetch you a clip over the earhole. See?"

"Yes, sir," Munro replied mildly.

On Camouflage, and Ships' Names

Captain D Bone

EARLY IN THE WAR the rappel of 'Business as usual' was as deadly at sea as elsewhere. Arrogant and super-confident in our pride of sea-place, we made little effort to trim and adapt our practice to rapidly altering conditions; there were few visible signs to disquiet us, we hardly deviated from our peaceful sea-path, and, had no concern for interference. We carried our lights ablaze, advertised our doings in plain wireless, announced our sailings and arrivals, and even devoted more than usual attention to keeping our ships as span in brave new paint and glistening varnish as the hearts of impressionable passengers could desire. .

We had difficulties with our manning. The seamen were off, at first tuck of drum, to what they reckoned a more active part in the great game of war – the strictly Naval Service – and we were left. with weak crews of new and raw hands to carry on the sea-trade. So, from the very first of it, we engaged in a moral camouflage in our efforts to keep up appearances, and show the neutrals with whom we did business that such a thing as war could hardly disturb the smooth running of our master machine – the Merchants' Service!

Some there were among us who saw the peril in such prominence, and took modest (and somewhat hesitating) steps to keep out of the limelight, by setting lonely courses on the sea, restraining the comradely gossip of wireless operators, and toning down appearances from brilliant polish to the more sombre part suiting a sea in war-time. Deck lights were painted over and obscured, funnel and masts were allowed to grey to neutral tints, the brown ash that discomposes fine paint at sea was looked upon with a new and friendly eye. The bias of chief mates (in a service where promotion is the due for a clean and tidy ship) was, with difficulty, overcome, and a new era of keen look-out and sea-trim started.

There was but moderate support for these bold iconoclasts who dared thus to affront our high fetish. Ship painting and decoration and upkeep were sacrosanct rites that even masters must conform to; the enactments of the Medes and Persians were but idle rules, mere by-laws, compared to the formulae and prescriptions that governed the tone of our pantry cupboards and the shades of cunning grain-work. We were peaceful merchantmen; what was the use of our dressing up like a parish-rigged man-o'-war? As to the lights – darkening ship would upset the passengers; there would be rumours and apprehension. They would travel in less 'nervous' vessels!

The mine that shattered *Manchester Commerce* stirred the base of our happy conventions; the cruise of the *Emden* set it swaying perilously; the torpedoes that sank *Falaba* and *Lusitania* blew the whole sham edifice to the winds, and we began to think of our ships in other terms than those of freight and passenger rates. Our conceptions of peaceful merchantmen were not the enemy's!

We set about to make our vessels less conspicuous. Grey! We painted our hulls and funnels grey. In many colours of grey. The nuances of our coatings were accidental. Poor quality paint and variable untimely mixings contributed, but it was mainly by crew troubles (deficiency and incapacity) that we came by our first camouflage. As needs must, we painted sections at a time – a patch here, a plate or two there – laid on in the way that real sailors would call 'inside-out'! We sported suits of many colours, an infinite variety of shades. Quite suddenly we realized that grey, in such an ample range – red-greys, blue-greys, brown-greys, green-greys – intermixed on our hulls, gave an excellent low-visibility colour that blended into the misty northern landscape.

Bolshevik now in our methods, we worked on other schemes to trick the murderer's eye. Convention again beset our path. The great god Symmetry – whom we had worshipped to our undoing – was torn from his high place. The glamour of Balances, that we had thought so fine and shipshape, fell from our eyes, and we saw treachery in every regular disposition. Pairs – in masts, ventilators, rails and stanchions, boat-groupings, samson posts, even in the shrouds and rigging – were spies to the enemy, and we rearranged and screened and altered as best we could, in every way that would serve to give a false indication of our course and speed. Freighters and colliers (that we had scorned because of ugly forward rake of mast and funnel) became the leaders of our fashion. We wedged our masts forward (where we could) and slung a gaff on the fore side of the foremast; we planked the funnel to look more or less upright; we painted a curling bow wash over the propeller and a black elaborate stern on the bows. We trimmed our ships by the head, and flattered ourselves that, Janus-like, we were heading all ways!

Few, including the enemy, were greatly deceived. At that point where alterations of apparent course were important – to put the putting Fritz off his stroke – the deck-houses and erections with their beamwise fronts or ends would be plainly noted, and a true line of course be readily deduced. With all our new zeal, we stopped short of altering standing structures, but we could paint, and we made efforts to shield our weakness by varied applications. Our device was old enough, a return to the chequer of ancient sea-forts and the line of painted gunports with which we used to decorate our clipper sailing ships. (That also was a camouflage of its day – an effort to overawe Chinese and Malay pirates by the painted resemblance to the gun-deck of a frigate.) We saw the eye-disturbing value of a bold criss-cross, and those of us who had paint to spare made a 'Hobson-jobson' of awning spars and transverse bulkheads.

These were our sea-efforts – rude trials effected with great difficulty in the stress of the new sea-warfare. We could only see ourselves from a surface point of view, and, in our empirics, we had no official assistance. During our brief stay in port it was impossible to procure day-labouring gangs – even the 'gulls' of the dockside were busy at sea. On a voyage, gun crews and extra look-outs left few hands of the watch available for experiments; in any case, our rationed paint covered little more than would keep the rust in check. We were relieved when new stars of marine coloration arose, competent shore concerns that, on Government instruction, arrayed us in a novel war paint. Our rough and amateurish tricks gave way to the ordered schemes of the dockyard; our ships were armed for us in a protective coat of many colours.

Upon us like an avalanche came this real camouflage. Somewhere behind it all a genius of pantomimic transformation blazed his rainbow wand and fixed us. As we came in from sea, dazzle-painters swarmed on us, bespattered creatures with no bowels of compassion, who painted over our cherished glass and teak-wood and brass port-rims – the last lingering evidences of our gentility. Hourly we watched our trim ships take on the hues of a swingman's roundabouts. We learned of fancy colours known only in high art – alizarin and grey-pink, purple-lake and Hooker's green. The designs of our mantling held us in a maze of expectation. Bends and ecartelés, indents and rayons, gyrony and counter-flory, appeared on our topsides; curves and arrow-heads were figured on boats and davits and deck fittings; apparently senseless dabs and patches were measured and imprinted on funnel curve and rounding of the ventilators; inboard and outboard we were streaked and crossed and curved.

With our arming of guns there was need for instruction in their service and maintenance; artificial smoke-screens required that we should be efficient in their use; our Otters called for some measure of seamanship in adjustment and control. So far all governmental appliances for our defence relied on our understanding and operation, but this new protective coloration, held. aloof from our confidence, it was quite self-contained, there was no rule to be learnt; we were to be shipmates with a new contrivance, to the operation of which we had no control. For want of point in discussion, we criticized freely. We surpassed ourselves in adjectival review; we stared in horror and amazement as each newly bedizened vessel passed down the river. In comparison and simile we racked memory for text to the gaudy creations. "Water running under a bridge." ... "Forced draught on a woolly sheep's back." ... "Mural decoration in a busy butcher's shop." ... "Strike *me* a rosy bloody pink!" said one of the hands, "if this 'ere don't remind me o' jaundice an' malaria an' a touch o' th' sun, an' me in a perishin' dago 'orspittel!"

While naming the new riot of colour grotesque – a monstrosity, an outrage, myopic madness – we were ready enough to grasp at anything that might help us in the fight at sea. We scanned our ships from all points and angles to unveil the hidden imposition. Fervently we hoped that there would be more in it than met our eye – that our preposterous livery was not only an effort to make Gargantuan faces at the Boche! Only the most splendid results could justify our bewilderment.

Out on the sea we came to a better estimate of the value of our novel war-paint. In certain lights and positions we seemed to be steering odd courses – it was very difficult to tell accurately the line of a vessel's progress. .The low visibility that we seamen had sought was sacrificed to enhance a bold disruption of perspective. While our efforts at deception, based more or less on a one colour scheme of greys, may have rendered our ships less visible against certain favouring backgrounds of sea and sky, there were other weather conditions in which we would stand out sharply revealed. Abandoning the effort to cloak a stealthy sea-passage, our newly constituted Department of Marine Camouflage decked us out in a bold pattern, skilfully arranged to disrupt our perspective, and give a false impression of our line of course. With a torpedo travelling to the limit of its run – striking anything that may lie in its course, range is of little account. Deflection, on the other hand, is everything in the torpedoman's problem – the correct estimation of a point of contact of two rapidly moving bodies. He relies for a solution on an accurate judgment of his target's course; it became the business of the dazzle-painters to complicate his working by a feint in colour and design. The new camouflage has so distorted our sheer and disrupted the colour in the mass as to make our vessels less easy to hit. If not invisible against average backgrounds, the dazzlers have done their work so well that we are at least partially lost in every elongation.

The mystery withheld from us – the system of our decoration – has done much to ease the rigours of our war-time sea-life. In argument and discussion on its origin and purpose we have found a topic, almost as unfailing in its interest as the record day's run of the old sailing ships. We are agreed that it is a brave martial coat we wear, but are divided in our theories of production. How is it done? By what shrewd system are we controlled that no two ships, are quite alike in their splendour? We know that instructions come from a department of the Admiralty to the dockyard painters, in many cases by telegraph. Is there a system of abbreviations, a colourist's shorthand, or are there maritime Heralds in Whitehall who blazon our arms for the guidance of the rude dockside painters? It can be worked out in fine and sonorous proportions:

For S.S. CORNCRIX

Party per pale, a pale; first, gules, a fesse dancette, sable; second, vert, bendy, lozengy, purpure cottised with nodules of the first; third, sable, three billets bendwise in fesse, or: sur tout de tout, a barber's pole cockbilled on a sinking gasometer, all proper. For motto: "Doing them in the eye."

One wonders if our old conservatism, our clinging to the past, shall persist long after the time of strife has gone; if, in the years when war is a memory and the time comes to deck our ships in pre-war symmetry and grace of black hulls and white-painted deck-work and red funnels and all the gallant show of it, some old masters among us may object to the change.

"Well, have it as you like," they may say. "I was brought up in the good old-fashioned cubist system o' ship painting – fine patterns o' reds an' greens an' Ricketts' blue, an' brandy-ball stripes an' that! None o' your damned newfangled ideas of one-colour sections for me! ... Huh! ... And black hulls, too! ... Black! A funeral outfit! ... No, sir! I may be wrong, but anyway, I'm too old now to chop and change about!"

If we have become reconciled to the weird patterns of our war-paint, every instinct of seafaring that is in us rebels against the new naming of our ships.

Is it but another form of camouflage – like the loving Indian mother abusing her dear children for deception of a malicious listening Djinn? *War Cowslip,*

War Dance, War Dreamer! War Hell! Are our new standard ships being thus badly named, that the enemy may look upon them as pariahs, unworthy of shell or torpedo? Perhaps, as a thoughtful war measure, it may be chargeful of pregnant meaning; our new war names for the ships may be germane to some distant world movement, the first tender shoot of which we cannot yet recognize! More than likely, it is the result of the fine war-time frolic of fitting the cubest of square pegs in the roundest of holes. How is it done? Is there, in the hutments of St. James's Park, an otherwise estimable and blameless greengrocer, officially charged with the task of finding names for vessels, 015537-68 inclusive, presently on the Controller's lists and due to be launched?

We sailors are jealous for our vessels. Abuse us if you will, but have a care for what you may say of our ships. We alone are entitled to call them bitches, wet brutes, stubborn craft, but we will stand for no such liberties from the beach; strikes have occurred on very much less sufficient ground. Ridicule in the naming of our ships is intolerable. If *War* is to be the prefix, why cannot our greengrocer find suitable words in the chronicles of strife? Can there be anything less martial than the *War Rambler, War Linnet, War Titmouse, War Gossamer*? Why not the *War Teashop*, the *War Picture House*, the – the – the *War Lollipop*? Are we rationed in ships' names? Is there a Controller of Marine Nomenclature? The thing is absurd!

If our controllers had sense they would see the .danger in thus flouting our sentiment; they would value the recruiting agency of a good name; they would recognize that the naming of a ship should be done with as great care as that of an heir to an earldom. Is the torpedoed bos'n of the *Eumaeus* going to boast of a new post on the *War Bandbox*? What are the feelings of the captain of a *Ruritania* when he goes to the yards to take over a *War Whistler*? Why *War*? If sober, businesslike argument be needed, it is confusing; it introduces a repetition of initial syllable that makes for dangerous tangles in the scheme of direction and control.

It is all quite unnecessary. There are names and enough. Fine names! Seamanlike names! Good names! Names that any sailor would be proud to have on his worsted jersey! Names that he would shout out in the marketplace! Names that the enemy would read as monuments to his infamy! Names of ships that we knew and loved and stood by to the bitter end.

I Was There

Nicholas Monsarrat
Copyright © The Estate of Nicholas Monsarrat 1958

SHE WAS A LOVELY boat, and a thousand times during that long trip across the Channel and up the French coast from Southampton to Flushing I found myself wishing she were mine. But country lawyers in a small way of business don't own sixty-ton diesel-powered yawls like the *Ariadne*: if they are lucky, they get the job of delivering them from their builders to other, more fortunate people. That was what I was doing that June evening, and not hurrying the job either; we had a fortnight to make the trip, ironing out the snarls on the way, and none of us wanted to cut that fortnight short.

'Us' was three people altogether: myself, on holiday from the dry-as-dust legal business of an English market town; George Wainwright, about whom I knew nothing save that he was on the fringe of London's theatrical world, and an excellent small-boat navigator; and Ginger, who tripled as steward, deck-hand, and running commentator. "Call me Ginger!" he had said in a cheerful Cockney voice as soon as we met on the dockside: "My mother was scared by a carrot!"

I had left it at 'Ginger'; he was the kind of man who

didn't need a second name.

This was the sort of holiday I took every year, signing on with a yacht-delivery service and pulling strings to wangle the best boat and the best trip I could. It was the only way I could get to sea nowadays; the war had taken my own boat, and the post-war my bank balance. George Wainwright told me, airily, that he was 'resting between shows', though I fancy he was glad enough to pick up free quarters and twenty pounds for making what was virtually a pleasure cruise. He was a big man, sinewy and tough. I had the impression that he had done a lot of ocean-racing at one time in other people's boats, though I couldn't imagine him in any conceivable part in any West End play.

Ginger, the steward, didn't volunteer anything about himself. He never stopped talking, for all that.

The crew on these 'builder's delivery' jobs was usually a scratch lot, though it struck me that this time we were remarkably assorted. Middle-aged lawyer, forty-year-old actor, a red-headed Cockney who might have been fresh out of jail – the crew of the *Ariadne* seemed to have been picked at random from the Yellow Pages. But we had made her sail like a champion, all the same.

We had made her sail to such good purpose that now, with two days in hand, we were loafing along on the last hundred miles of the journey. Earlier, we had come smoking up the Channel before a Force 6 gale; *Ariadne*, handling beautifully, had logged a steady ten knots under her storm canvas. But then the wind had fallen light, and the leg from Dover to Calais had become a. gentle drifting under hazy sunshine, while the decks and the sails dried out and we made what small repairs were necessary. Nothing had gone wrong that didn't always go wrong in a boat fresh from the builders – a leaking skylight, some chafed rigging, a cupboard door that wouldn't stay shut in a seaway. By and large, she went like a dream – as far as I was concerned, an envious dream of ownership that I would never live in reality.

George Wainwright and I had taken turn-about at the wheel, with Ginger filling in for an odd trick or two to give us an extra margin of sleep. We had lived on tea, corned beef, beans, and something which Ginger called 'cheesy-hammy-eggy', and which, for cold, hungry, and tired men, was a banquet in itself. Rum, twice a day, completed our paradise.

Now, towards the end of that paradise, we were punching eastwards against the ebb tide at six o'clock of a magic evening. *Ariadne*, under all plain sail, could not make much of the light air; we were barely holding our own, creeping up the flat coastline with the sun warm on our backs. I had the wheel, letting the spokes slide through my fingers with a sensual joy. Ginger, standing with his head poking out of the cabin top, was drying cups and saucers. George Wainwright, his elbows planted on the chart, stared landwards through his binoculars.

"We're not making any headway," he said presently. "Barely a knot, I should say."

"Suits me," said Ginger irrepressibly. He could never resist a comment on anything, from UN politics to juvenile delinquency. "I've got all year."

The water gurgled at the bow. The sail slatted, empty of wind.

"We might as well anchor," I said. "The tide will be

against us for another four hours. What's the depth here?"

George Wainwright glanced at the chart. "About four fathoms. Sandy bottom. She'll hold all right."

"We'll anchor till the flood," I decided. "Give us a chance to catch up on our sleep," I eased *Ariadne* up into the wind, and our way fell off. Ginger went forward to see to the windlass. "How far are we off shore?" I asked George.

"About a mile," he answered. "The tide sets us inwards,"

"And where, exactly?"

"Off Dunkirk,"

Dunkirk ... As the anchor-chain rattled down through the leads, and *Ariadne* swung and settled to her cable, I was conscious of an odd foreboding. It was true that we were a mile off Dunkirk: I recognized, as if from a hundred photographs, the oily swell, the sloping beaches, the flat mainland enclosing a loose-knit grey town. Here were the waters, full of ghosts, full of sunken ships and dead men, which a decade earlier — no, it was now nearly *two* decades — had resounded to a. murderous uproar. In my mind's eye I saw them all again; the straggling lines of men wading through the shallows, crying out for rescue or waiting in dull stupor to be picked up: the burning town behind, the Stukas overhead, and the small boats darting in and out — going in light, coming out laden to the gunwales — on an errand of mercy and salvage that went on hour after hour, day after day. That was what Dunkirk would always mean to me — a name at once grisly and proud, a symbol, a haunting from the past. I was curious to know what it meant to the other two, and I did not have to wait long to find out.

Ginger, having secured the anchor, came aft again. George Wainwright looked up from his chart, where *Ariadne*'s observed position was now marked by a neatly pencilled cross. There was no need to wonder which of them would speak first. It would have been an easy bet to win.

"Good old Dunkirk!" said Ginger jauntily. He wiped his hands, greasy from the windlass, on a bunch of cotton-waste, and looked round him at *Ariadne*'s benevolent anchorage. "Makes you think a bit, don't it?"

"How do you mean, Ginger?" asked George Wainwright.

"All this ..." Ginger waved his hand round vaguely.

"It's nineteen years ago now, but by cripes it's like yesterday! ... The bombers coming over as thick as bloody fleas, the lads waiting ... I'll never forget it, not as long as I live. By cripes, skipper I" he turned to me, his creased leathery face alight, "I could tell you a yarn that would curl your hair! A yarn ..."

... A yarn which, as the sun sank to the westwards, and *Ariadne*'s wavering shadow lengthened and faded on the; tranquil waters off Dunkirk, recalled all the horrors, terrors, and triumphs of those mortal days. Ginger told it well; l knew that he must have had many audiences, many chances to polish and perfect.

'The lads, he said (and we could all see them as lads, beefy Lancashire lads from the mills, grey-faced lads from the Yorkshire coal pits, likely lads from Bermondsey and Bow) the lads were fed up. The officer had promised them they'd be taken off that night, and they'd been content with that, after a week's dodging the bombers on their way back to the coast, and they'd settled down on the beach to wait. But they hadn't been taken off, not that night, nor the next, nor the next. That was the army for you – waiting about, nobody knowing what was happening, all a lot of bull, put that bloody light out! ... First they had waited on the beach; then at the water's edge; then chest-high in the water itself.

The straggling line inched its way outwards from the shallows to the deep water. "Link arms, there!" said the officer; so they linked arms, and with the other hand held their rifles safely above water. "Because you'll be using those rifles tomorrow," said the officer. "Keep them dry, keep them ready for instant action!" "'Ark at 'im," said the lads ...

They waited in the shallows and the deeps. It was cold at night; then it was hot; behind them the town was burning, and the perimeter force kept blazing away with everything they'd got, and the Stukas circled, and swooped, and roared away again, leaving behind them a salty human flotsam – mixed with sand, men mixed with water, seaweed, other men, all draining slowly away as the tide ebbed. "Where's the bloody Air Force?" asked the lads, scanning the alien sky between waves of noise and pain. "Tucked up in bed with anyone they can get hold of" ... "Heard from your missus lately?..."

It was cold at night, then it was burning hot. Men got hit, and dropped out; men got cramp, and floated away; men went mad, and tried to hide beneath the waves. There were other straggling lines within sight, like feelers weaving and groping towards home. Their own line grew thinner; sometimes part of it disappeared altogether, as if by weight of noise and pressure. "Close up!" said the officer. "And no smoking there! Might give away our position."

The officer was the last to go. He was one of the lads himself, only a bit lah-di-dah ... When it was their turn to be taken off, the boat from the destroyer, bobbing inshore after a stick of bombs had straddled the shallows, drew alongside the wavering line. .

"Look lively!" said the sailor at the helm, as cool as fresh salad, and they looked lively – as lively as they could after three days of it. There was one lad going off his head with the noise and the sun, and he tried to clamber on board, suddenly screaming with mingled pain and joy, and the officer came up behind and gave him a heave into the boat, and then himself crumpled up like a sodden newspaper and disappeared without a trace.

They fished around for him, couldn't find him, suddenly abandoned the idea and drew softly away. Better to save twenty lives, they reassured themselves ... But it was funny how surprised he had looked after three such days, just before he faded out.

Dusk came down like a blessing. *Ariadne* rode to her anchor proudly; she was gleaming new, and the white of her doused sails seemed to hold the sunlight long after it had dipped below the horizon. I would have needed a lot of things – a lot of luck, a lot of horse-sense, a lot of drive I had never had – to possess a boat like this. But somehow, sitting relaxed in the cockpit, nursing a rum-and-water, I found it easy to imagine that it had all happened, and that she was mine.

The lights of Dunkirk were coming on one by one.

George Wainwright took an anchor-bearing from them, satisfied himself that we were not dragging, and sat down by my side again. He raised his voice against the lap and gurgle of the tideway.

"That was a good yarn of yours, Ginger," he said. "I know exactly how you must have felt ... But it was just as bad for the little ships that had to come close inshore and take the troops off. If you want to hear a story ..."

...A story about a big man in a small boat (and, looking at George Wainwright's broad shoulders as he lounged at the after-end of the cockpit, we both knew that it was his story.) Hundreds of little ships played their part in the evacuation of Dunkirk; everything from old paddle-wheel ferries to ship's lifeboats, nursed across the Channel by a man and a boy. Their job was to run a shuttle service – to come close inshore, load up with troops, and bring them out to deeper water where the bigger boats and the destroyers were waiting.

Some of the little ships kept it up for three or four days. The two-and-a-half-ton sloop *Tantivvy* was one of these.

Tantivvy (said George Wainwright) was nothing to look at though she was the owner's pride and joy. She'd sailed across from Dover with the rest of the mob, following a call on the radio which asked for every small ship that could stay afloat to report for emergency duty. The motley fleet fanned out like a crazy Armada, then converged on Dunkirk. Dunkirk, with its pall of smoke, its mass of shipping, its hurricane of gunfire, was something you couldn't miss.

Tantivvy, drawing less than four feet, could get within half a mile of the shore; and there she anchored, and presently launched from her upper deck a small pram-dinghy propelled by a large man whose bulk left room for, at the very most, two other passengers ... All day, and most of the night, the dinghy plied to and fro, taking off two soldiers at a time from the waiting hordes, loading them on to the deck of *Tantivvy*, and then going back for more.

There came a time, towards dawn, when *Tantivvy* had fifty passengers. They sprawled in the tiny cabin, grey-faced, dead to the world; they lay about on the upper deck, soiling it with their blood; they sat with their backs to the mast, staring at nothing, waiting for peace. After his twenty-fifth trip; the big man looked at them, and said: "Not many more, I'm afraid."

One of the soldiers, still awake and still able to talk, waited for a lull in the bombing, and called out: "Let's get going, for God's sake!"

"We might manage two more," said the big man, resting his swollen, aching arms on the oars.

"Don't be a bloody fool!" said the soldier in a cracked voice. "You'll lose the lot of us if you do. We're damn near sinking already."

A· bomb fell with a screaming crump! and a shower of dirty· water, close beside them.

"Well ..." said the big man. His face was deadly tired, his eyes puffy and discoloured.

He climbed on board, secured the dinghy to the stern post, and started up the tiny motor.

"Help me with the anchor," he said to the soldier.

The two of them shambled forwards; picking their way between half-dead men who, even when kicked out of the way, could not spare them a glance. They heaved on the anchor and finally brought it home. The big man stood upright, and then suddenly stiffened.

"You stupid bastard!" he said to the soldier.

"What?" said the soldier, in amazement.

There was an enormous explosion ashore, and the small boat, gathering way, rocked as the hot shock-wave reached them.

"Don't you know better," asked the big man, with murderous sarcasm, "than to walk on a wooden deck in those blasted hobnailed boots?"

There was a breeze coming up from the southward, sending the small ripples slap-slapping against *Ariadne*'s shapely hull. An hour before moonrise, it was now very dark; Dunkirk's glow was· reflected in the sky overhead, but between the town and the boat there was a waste of inky black water, deserted, featureless. It was as if the soldiers had all been picked up, and we were free to go ...

In the glow from the binnacle Ginger's perky face was sombre. Perhaps, for him as well, the ghosts were still thick around us. If only for our comfort I knew that I had to tell them about the triumphant part, the end of the story ...

... The end of the story, which I could see now, as clearly as the others had seen theirs.

She was an old destroyer, a bit cranky in her ways (which were the ways of 1916, not 1940) and bringing her alongside at Dover, feverishly crammed with shipping, was not easy. Not if you'd been on the bridge for thirty-six hours, and made two trips to Dunkirk, and dodged the bombers all the way there and all the way back, and waited off-shore, sweating, while eight hundred and sixty-two men scrambled, clawed, and bullocked their way on board. Not if you had to go back, as soon as this lot was landed, and do the whole thing over and over again till there were no more soldiers showing above water.

The old destroyer slipped between two trawlers leaving for a routine minesweep, stopped in her tracks with a sudden boiling of foam aft, and edged sideways towards the quay. The lines went snaking ashore, the windlasses took in the slack; presently she was berthed, and the hum of the main engines ceased. The captain walked to the back of the bridge and looked aft along the length of his ship.

This was the dividend, this was what the excursion had been for .... There wasn't an inch of the deck that was not covered with men – men in khaki. On the trip home they had lain there as though stunned or dead; now they were stirring, moving towards the gangway and peering down at the Dover dockside as if they could scarcely believe their eyes. Their uniforms were filthy, their faces unshaven, their many bandages bloodstained; they looked like a wretched scarecrow army in some hollow Shakespearian comedy. About half of them had rifles. There was no other equipment.

The destroyer captain thought: if this is what's left of the British Army, then God help us ...

They began to disembark, shambling down the gangplank like men sleepwalking in a dream of death. They collected in groups, and then in ragged lines, filling the whole quayside. There was a bunch of them directly below the bridge, standing as if in a shattered trance.

Then suddenly one of them, a small lance-corporal,

looked up at the bridge, and then directly at the destroyer captain himself. For a moment they held each other's eyes as if they were seeking some rare, unheard-of element that could bridge the ground between a stunted Cockney soldier and a tall, beribboned Royal Navy captain; and then the small lance-corporal grinned, and looked round at his weary comrades, and shouted, on a cracked note of energy:

"Come on, lads! Three cheers for the bleedin' Nyvy!" They could hardly be called three cheers; they were like the thin rise and fall of a groan, or a spectral sighing from an army of ghosts. But they did emanate from those bedraggled ranks, and they did reach the gaunt, teak-faced destroyer captain on the bridge.

The captain, when he went ashore, was the elder son of an earl; and, when afloat, an unbending disciplinarian who had been known to deal out exemplary punishment for a sloppy salute. It was a difficult moment, covered by no textbook, no family code, and indeed no war so far. But he also had something important to express, and he did the best he could. He leant over the wing of his bridge, stiff as a rod in spite of his weariness, and enunciated very clearly:

"My compliments to *you*, gentlemen – my *best* compliments,"

They liked my story, I could tell that; it reminded them that the Dunkirk disaster could be read two ways. In the binnacle glow, Ginger's face grew cheerful again, and George Wainwright took a swig of his rum as if toasting Victory herself. The night breeze, from landwards, brought a warm homely smell of Flanders fields. At anchor off Dunkirk we had mourned long enough; for the tragedy had a happy ending, after all.

"That's what we tend to forget," said George, echoing my thoughts. "We *did* take off more than three hundred thousand of them, and they *did* get back again, in the end."

Looking up after the long spell of talking, I became aware that the lights of Dunkirk were no longer on *Ariadne*'s starboard beam, but traversing slowly round astern of her. The Channel tide was flooding.

"We're swinging, skipper," said George Wainwright, noticing at the same moment. "The tide's with us now. The wind's got some weight in it, too,"

I clicked the switch of the navigation lights, and the friendly red and green eyes brought *Ariadne* to life.

"Let's get under way," I said.

"Now you're talking I" said Ginger. "This place gives me the creeps."

We were all standing up, ready to go about our tasks – hoisting the foresail and the main, getting up the anchor, putting ourselves and *Ariadne* to work again.

"Of course Dunkirk is haunted," said George Wainwright suddenly. "But it gave us something to be proud of, all the same."

Some quality of wistfulness in his voice prompted me to ask a question which had been in my mind ever since the three of us started talking.

"Tell me something," I said ."*Were* you at Dunkirk?"

It was light enough to see him grin. "Not actually, old boy," he answered. Suddenly *he* did sound like an actor, rather a good one. "I was touring with ENSA at the time. *Private Lives*-eight shows a week. I wasn't actually *at* Dunkirk,"

It seemed right that he did not sound sheepish .... I turned towards the slight figure clambering up to the fo'c'sle deck.

"Ginger? Were you?"

"Not me!" I might have been charging him with picking pockets. "1940, wasn't it?-I was in the glasshouse already! Asleep on sentry-go, the man said. What a — liberty!"

I knew what was coming next.

"Were *you* there?" George Wainwright asked me.

I didn't want to embarrass either of them; in any case, I couldn't be sure that, even now, they were telling the truth. One of them was an actor, the other a liar; they lived, congenitally, in opposite corners of the same dream-world. And I myself led such a dull life nowadays ...

"Afraid not," I answered. "Bad heart, you know ... I was doing civil defence work in London all that summer. I wasn't at Dunkirk either,"

But the moment of revelation did not make us ashamed among ourselves, nor were we truly liars, whether we were lying or not. For our last three answers had all been wrong. Every Englishman was at Dunkirk.

Without Incident

G. Drake

THIS IS NO STORY of loss by enemy action, of peril by submarine attack, of surface raiders or aircraft hunting us over the wide seas. It is just a story of the everyday hazards the seaman must overcome if he is to do his part in this war for the four freedoms.

It all started in New York's North River when, after a week's waiting for our convoy to collect in weather below zero, we hove up our anchors to go down to the Examination Anchorage where we would await Captain Briggs's return from the convoy conference. The port anchor came up crown first, with two shackles of cable in a hurrah's nest of bights and hitches fouling the flukes and a twenty-five-foot spar sticking through the middle of it like a skewer through chickens' livers. I had visions of having to get a barge to clear the tangle, and the delay would mean that we should miss the convoy, and I cursed the pilot who had ordered that anchor to be dropped while we were still going full ahead.

We let go the starboard anchor off Staten Island an hour before dark that afternoon. As soon as we had brought up, I turned out the watch below to help clear the mess. I'll not bother you with details of how we got that spar out and hung off the anchor with turns of mooring wire while we sorted out the hitches of cable. We could not send a man over the side in a bos'n's chair, for if he had got a foot or a hand into a loose bight and the chain slipped I should have been to blame, and, more important, the ship would have been a hand short. We had no hands to spare. Just as the Old Man returned from the conference with Sparks we got the job done and the anchor hove right up.

We had hoped to be vice-commodore of the convoy, for that would have meant two naval signalmen to attend to all convoy signals, and they augment that most vital part of the convoy's make-up, the look-outs. Our hopes died quickly when Captain Briggs came up the Jacob's ladder. We were not even to be a column leader. We were stuck at the tail of No. 7 column until the convoy arrived off the Western Approaches, where it would split up into smaller groups, each for a different destination, when we were to be commodore of the Liverpool section. Captain Briggs did not like it. Neither did we, though for other reasons. The Old Man did not like being made commodore of anything at all. He said that if they paid him the £1700 a year that was the regular commodore's salary he would do the job gladly, but to ask him to shoulder the responsibility for other ships besides his own for nothing but the problematic satisfaction of doing the job efficiently was not good enough. He had had some before, he said, and it had been too much for him. I knew what he meant. When we were at sea in the danger area (and God knows there was not much of the Western Ocean that was not a danger area) he could not reconcile it with his conscience to peel off and turn in to his bunk. He would sleep, all standing, either in his arm-chair or on his settee, getting infrequent cat-naps of an hour or so for twenty days on end, and longer if we ran into bad weather. For three and a half years he had been doing it now, with a week or so at home perhaps twice in the year, and the strain was beginning to tell. He was growing thinner, and his manner was often nervously brusque where once it had been – well, suave is the word that best describes it. His rather sad, sallow face, with its long forehead and close crown of grey hair, looked too fine-drawn. The Articles said he was forty-nine, but he looked nearer sixty. And because I liked him and was sorry for him, as well as because it was my job, I was determined that I would carry as much as I could of that extra responsibility which had been so gratuitously unloaded upon him.

From harbour to the fiftieth meridian took a week, for the speed of a convoy is the speed of its slowest member; a week of freezing weather. The moon was in its first quarter, and in the first watch each night the ships glittered like diamonds scattered on a polished floor, as the moonlight was reflected from the ice which plastered hull and rail and superstructure. In other circumstances I might have felt my pulse quicken with the sheer beauty of it all. As it was, I swore at the gleaming splendour which might betray us to enemy eyes. But nothing happened except that the bos'n slipped and sprained his ankle, so depriving me of my only day worker, and putting a stop to all maintenance work.

Once we cleared the Grand Banks of Newfoundland

the cold vanished, giving place to a warm blanket of fog. The uninitiated might think fog a beneficent concealment to a big convoy, but it concealed our adversary from us much more than it concealed us from our adversary. At dawn one day we heard the scattering of a pattern of depth charges from a wing escort, but we were too intent on maintaining contact with an invisible and inaudible next-ahead to be able to spare it much attention. Even in clear weather that heterogeneous collection of ships of all sizes, types, and speeds called a convoy requires that each individual shall make constant adjustment to course and speed to maintain position relative to the next-ahead and the next-astern so that the convoy can always act as a unit in emergency. In fog each ship, except those at the tail of the column, towed a specially constructed wooden plane which threw up a white spout of water as a mark and a warning to the next-astern, but in that flat, uncertain half light of drifting grey vapour there was neither shape nor colour, and even the fog-buoys were almost invisible. Fog is always; to the seaman, something of a strain, but in convoy – peering, listening, tensed to take immediate action to avoid collision – it was more like a nightmare. This sort of thing lasted a week, and then, under the influence of a falling glass and a freshening south-west wind, the fog cleared to a thin drizzle. Of our original number eleven had vanished, silently and without fuss. I shall never know whether they had just straggled, or whether they had met the hidden adversary. It is so easy to lose contact in a fog that I hope they may have made port before we did.

For the following two days the wind piped up from

the south-west until the bunting stood out from the halliards like boards when the commodore passed his signals. We had neither sun nor stars from which to get a true position and so check our dead reckoning, that estimate of our position worked out from our last certain observation off Cape Race in Newfoundland, which might easily be several miles in error owing to the uncertain set of the Gulf Stream Drift and to leeway. We could not check our compass error. We navigated by guess and by God. In normal weather we took observations of stars at dawn and twilight, and of the sun for longitude in the morning and afternoon and for latitude at apparent noon, and so kept a continuous record of the ship's progress. The error accumulating from day to day when observations could not be taken might have little consequence in the wider expanses of the ocean, but when it came to making a landfall at night, on a coast where the majority of lighthouses were now extinguished, a very few miles might mean the difference between safety and disaster. For a shipmaster concerned only with his own ship this was worry enough. But now, on the second day of the sou'-west gale, the signal came down for us to change places with the leader of the starboard wing column which consisted of the Liverpool ships, and we knew that the moment was coming when our responsibility would include their safety and guidance.

The Old Man spent the next hour in a close study of the chart of "The Western Approaches to the Firth of Clyde," which includes the channels between the north-western part of Ireland and the Hebrides, and the North Channel between Rathlin Island and the Mull of Kintyre. When he came on top (he always kept the meal relief in the first dog watch) his startlingly blue eyes looked anxious. We discussed the possibility of our being ahead of our dead reckoning and perhaps to the northward, since the present wind would accelerate the normal rate of the Gulf Stream Drift. I said I thought it was too early to worry about it just yet. The glass must start to rise some time, and then the wind would shift to nor'west, bringing clear intervals and a possibility of getting a fix by sun or stars. But I had to admit that there was not much sign of it rising yet, which was but poor comfort to Captain Briggs. As we stood at the bridge-rail I caught sight of the second mate going down the port ladder with the brass sheath and a can of arming tallow for the patent sounding machine, and I felt pleased. It is cheering to see a young fellow doing his job without being told to do it, and young Maltby had been only a dog watch at sea, as the shellback would say. We were approaching the bank of soundings, the Continental Shelf where the deep water of the Atlantic shoals up to our coastal waters, and where it is possible with a twenty-eight pound weight at the end of three hundred fathoms of fine wire to lower a glass tube, coated inside with chromate of silver and open only at the lower end, to the bottom of the sea. As pressure increases in direct proportion to the depth, water is forced into the tube, changing the chromate into chloride, and thus by the change of colour recording the depth. Our old ship had none of the modern navigational instruments such as echo sounding or radio direction finding, but we did have a little electrically driven sounding machine of this type which worked very well when it did not break down, and we hoped it would reserve its caprice for the shore electrician who would have it to overhaul in Liverpool. When I went below at half-past eight, the Old Man was still poring over the chart. I could not help him, so I went to bed.

When I relieved Maltby at four in the morning it was as black as the inside of a black cat. He said the Old Man was resting in his arm-chair and I was to stamp on the deck if I wanted him. I could faintly discern the screw-wash of the wing escort corvette. I checked the course as nearly as I could. Ships in the neighbouring columns were completely invisible, but some poor devil over to port, probably the diesel tanker in No. 3, was blowing a shower of sparks out of her exhausts. It looked like the pillar of fire that led the Children of Israel. I hoped it would not lead their arch-enemies. Maltby and I had a steaming cup of cocoa which he had made in a little coffee percolator he kept in the chart-room, and then he went off on his rounds. We did that each watch, just to see that the blackout remained black, and that none of the lifeboats were working adrift in their griping bands.

It was half-past seven before the growing daylight revealed the dark smudges which were our neighbours. Slowly they became more certain in outline until, by eight o'clock, it was light enough to see the bunting standing stiffly out to port from the halliards of our next-abeam. Because the flags were blowing directly away from us that signal was difficult to read, but I knew it by heart. It was the signal we awaited. "Liverpool section proceed to your destination independently." The Old Man must have been on the look-out for it, too, for as I put the glasses down I found him beside me.

"A hundred and five miles to Altacarry Head, and it's dark at half-past five," I heard him say. "If we make them do nine and we're a bit ahead of our reckoning, we might just make a landfall before dark. I wish he would hurry up and haul down that hoist."

For most signals the executive is the hauling down of the commodore's hoist, and I could feel impatience stirring in Captain Briggs, like yeast in a bottle. Before I went down to breakfast I had the satisfaction of seeing the flags come fluttering down to be replaced by the usual hoists, "Station has been well kept," and "A safe passage and God speed," conventional signals from the commodore which we affect to despise, but which each of us secretly finds satisfying. After all, a difficult job has been well done.

But the more difficult part lay ahead. With our section's distinguishing signal flying at the triatic stay, and the Red Duster at the foremast-head, we led our eight ships off at a tangent, easing our speed to allow them to close up, though the Old Man chafed audibly and visibly at the necessity. I stayed around on the bridge, although I had reams of paper work to do below, for I knew the Old Man would want somebody to talk to. The young third mate, whose watch it was, was an unresponsive youth who held one of the wartime temporary second mate's certificates. He was inexperienced and not very tactful, and though far from being incompetent, was not the man to nurse Captain Briggs through a critical period of nervous strain. He was much more likely to precipitate an outburst of some sort, so I let the papers wait.

The wind still hung in the sou'-west, broad on the starboard quarter now and blowing pretty strong. By dead reckoning we should be on the bank of soundings, so I took the stand-by man down with me to the sounding machine. When I got back on the bridge ten minutes later we were walking along at a good nine knots; "sixty-five revs.". was chalked up on the inside of the wooden dodger. The glass tube from the sounding machine, read against the box-wood scale, gave fifty-six fathoms. We were on the bank sure enough, but you can get fifty-six fathoms from a point due west of Tory Island to the Stanton Bank, thirty-odd miles to the northward. We might be anywhere on that line, and the sky was overcast, and a thin drizzle was falling. The ships from which we had diverged so short a time ago were already mere phantoms to port, and even as I watched, became more spectral as the drizzle spread to the north, and finally vanished. Eight of us, accompanied by a corvette, were all that was visible inside the woolly ring of our horizon. Even the last ship in our little line, less than two miles astern of us, was only a dark grey blur in the universal grey cloud. We pressed on, hoping for the weather to clear enough to give us some sort of a landfall, but at noon when Maltby relieved the bridge it was still the same.

The flood stream runs due south, westward of Inishtrahull Island lighthouse, which was one of our hoped-for landfalls, and the ebb due north. As you make easting the streams trend farther to the east and west respectively, but their influence is modified to an unknown degree by the wind, which seemed to be falling a little, though the glass remained steady and there was no sign of a lift in the clouds. I plotted a course on the chart, allowing for these influences, to make Altacarry Head light on Rathlin Island 180 degrees, three miles. The Old Man eyed it for some moments, and noted a nineteen fathom patch north-west of Rathlin. He stepped it off with the dividers.

"We'll take a cast every half-hour from 1600 hours onward and hope for the best," he said. "We should pick up that patch somewhere between four-thirty and tea-time."

But we did not. At four-thirty the corvette appeared close aboard, and a crisp naval voice on the loud-hailer said, "Captain, you are now 360 degrees, eleven miles from Inishtrahull." Captain Briggs waved his arm in acknowledgment and thanks, and the second mate went into the chart-room to plot the bearing and see if it tallied with our sounding of thirty fathoms. It did. There were other places where we might have got the same depth, but the corvette, equipped with direction finder, or some other new device, would be pretty sure of his position before passing it on to us. We could do no better than rely on it. We hoisted a signal for our little fleet, warning them to watch us closely for alterations of course during the dark hours, and set a course for five miles north of Altacarry. With forty miles to go, and the stream setting westerly with a spring rate of three knots, it would be past ten o'clock before we reached the North Channel.

We plugged along, looking rather like a line of runner ducks, but making less noise. Somehow in that thickening light even the squawking of the black-headed gulls seemed to take on a quality of silence. Perhaps it was a result of strained nerves, but it was as if all echo were deadened, as though the damp and woolly air were too languid to carry sound at all, or too preoccupied in its hurry to get to Scotland. Chacun à son goût. I was in a hurry to get to Devon.

Captain Briggs relieved me for tea as usual, and by the time I returned to the bridge it was intensely dark. Being in our own backyard, as it were, we could, and did, burn dimmed navigation lights. The dimming was an unnecessary precaution. They could not have been visible at a cable's length on full power. But our next-astern would have warning from our stern light before she hit us behind, and would probably be able to see when we altered course.

Altacarry light shows normally twenty-two miles, but I doubted whether we should see it more than five miles in the murk which still drove up from the sou'-west. At eight when the third mate took over the bridge I went down to the chart-room to write up the log-book, and found the Old Man again studying the chart. The excitement of homecoming was seething in him, as indeed it was in all of us. We had a touch of what the shellback calls 'channel fever'. Unfortunately, in Captain Briggs it reinforced the strain to which his body and nerves were already subjected. His hand shook so that the dividers could not be relied upon to hold a stride of ten miles, and I had to step the distance off for him, making a tentative tick to represent our probable position at eight o'clock. Having decided that we should see the expected light before ten, we went back to the bridge together. Nothing was said, but he knew that I was going to stay there until we made a safe landfall.

You see, coming into that channel between Rathlin Island and the Isle of Islay in thick weather, if for any reason you overshoot your distance, either by overestimating an adverse tide or underestimating a favourable one, and you fail to see Altacarry, you are likely to be hard and fast on the Mull of Kintyre, before the lead gives you warning. We had allowed for a knot and a half of tide against us until about nine-thirty, and an hour of slack water before the south-east going stream should begin. But the spring rate might be anything between one and three knots, although it was probably nearer the lower limit being opposed to that continuous westerly wind. So, at nine o'clock we were peering into the gloom to starboard, hoping for a glimpse of Altacarry's quick flash. We saw nothing. There was nothing to see except the enveloping drizzle. At nine-thirty we saw nothing. At ten, nothing. Captain Briggs lowered his glasses and, without turning his head, said, "At ten-thirty I shall turn out to seaward if we don't see it by then." I was startled. Whether or not our line of ducks turned with us the duty we owed them would make us in some degree responsible for them, and if they, or some of them, decided to try to make port and one of them failed there would be inquiries and who knew what sort of trouble. With the wind abeam and the tide on the starboard bow we were likely enough to set so strongly to northward as to pass Altacarry at a range beyond the present limit of visibility, yet our position would be no whit bettered if we turned to seaward. There were other ships bound inward. There was an invisible shore on each side of us. And the weather might persist for days, or even weeks, and we should have the same gauntlet to run tomorrow or the next day, or the next ... But above all my mind dwelt upon the tide at four o'clock the next afternoon, and the Brunswick entrance standing open at the top of high water. We had no time to spare.

At twenty past ten, gazing earnestly into impenetrable mist, I said, "I think I see a light there, sir, about three points before the beam." Captain Briggs snatched up his glasses and followed my line of sight.

"Do you think you can get a bearing of it?" he said.

I tried, but without success. After we had docked the Old Man told me that he did not know whether I had dreamed that light, whether it was just another example of that now popular pastime, wishful thinking, or whether I really did see it. Nobody else saw it, and I did not see it again. All three of us looked longingly for it until eleven, when the third mate took another cast of the lead. He reported fifty fathoms.

The Middle Bank, I thought; so she has gone to the north like a crab. If we hold on for an hour and set as strongly south we should see the Mull ... "No! I can't see it now, sir," I answered the Old Man's question.

Then began a discussion which took almost all the· next half-hour. I felt that he wanted to be persuaded of the unwisdom of turning seaward, but that, with all his war-worn nerves crying out for safety and certitude, he would be difficult to convince. I used all the arguments I could reasonably advance, and some which were perhaps unreasonable. And I failed. At half-past eleven his mind was made up. We were to turn our backs on all that we had been looking forward to during these weary weeks, on everything we cared for.

"Go down and take a cast, Harrison," he said to the third mate, "and we'll see if we can plot some sort of departure position." Then turning to me, he said, "Signal our intention to our next-astern."

I picked up the night signalling torch to do what I had so little mind to, and as I stepped to the rail in the bridge wing out of that infernal green fuzz thrown by the starboard side light there came once again that crisp, that blessed voice.

"Captain, you are now nought twenty degrees, nine miles from Altacarry. You should alter your course forthwith."

And then I made my first boner. I dropped the signal torch from my nerveless hand and it was irreparably smashed.

It shows how much the Old Man wanted to hold on that he accepted the corvette's announcement without question, and acted upon the advice given. And in due course there flashed Altacarry light, but not until we were a bare two miles from it, and even then it was a whiskery kind of glim, a mere momentary brightening of the pervading drizzle. But as we drew farther under the lee of the land the visibility improved, and we were able to set our courses from point to point through the channel. The south-east-going stream was behind us, giving us even more help than its counterpart had done hindrance. I went to bed. As I passed the captain's door he was already asleep ... in his arm-chair. He was too tired to undress.

At four I relieved Maltby. The Mull of Galloway light was fine on the port quarter, and by daylight we were rounding the Chicken Rock lighthouse and tearing up Liverpool Bay like a scalded cat. We made the tide, of course, and there was Brunswick entrance standing open on the top of high water just as I had imagined it in the night. We towed into the dock with familiar faces on the river wall to greet us, and before dark were secure in our berth. It has all been described so often before that I will leave it to you to picture to yourself.

Captain Briggs was in that mood sometimes described as being above oneself. Had I not known how abstemious he always was I should have thought his merriness came out of a bottle. He spoke more warmly than was his wont; he smiled gaily; he looked ten years younger; he was going home.

I went over to the end of the shed to telephone my wife that I should not be home for a while yet; not until the cargo was discharged. After the first exchanges (and the first three minutes) were over, she asked, "What sort of a voyage did you have, darling?"

"Absolutely without incident, beloved," I replied. I am always strictly truthful.

Quiet Holiday With a Genius

Weston Martyr

I LIVE BY MYSELF in a little house in the depths of the country, miles away from anywhere. I live a very quiet life and see very few people. I like it.

Odo Hunter lives in a bustling, shipbuilding port on the other side of England, where he is extremely busy, knows everyone, and is never, never quiet. He likes it.

This will explain why I was astonished when, one fine day in the summer of 1944, Odo burst in upon me through the french window of my sitting-room and announced that he had come to stay with me for a week. He added, 'I've got the Missis and a lifeboat outside. What shall I do with 'em?'

As I do not want anyone to think Odo is mad, or was drunk, I had better explain at once that the man is a genius and does not think, behave, look, or talk like an ordinary person. If he did he would not be a genius. I do not imply that his strange behaviour, queer appearance, and unorthodox manner of expressing himself make him a genius. These things are merely the marks of the breed. What does make him a genius is the originality and speed of his thought. If a man paints better pictures, or composes better music than anyone else, we call him a genius. The things Odo creates fulfil their purpose better than the things created by other men to fulfil the same purpose. Odo creates — that is, designs and builds — better boats than anyone else, therefore I call him a genius.

When Odo mentioned the presence, outside, of a wife and a lifeboat I did not rise to his bait. I know my Odo, and I knew the delight he takes in pulling legs. I grinned and said, 'If you really have come to stay with me, I am delighted. But rations for one don't go very far, old fellow, so I hope you've brought some food along.' Whereat Odo rushed to the front door and roared, 'It's all right, Missis. He says he's delighted. I told you so.'

This time I did rise — in a hurry. Drawn up in the narrow lane outside my front gate I saw a big car, a small lady sitting placidly inside it, and, behind, a large, blue lifeboat on a trailer.

I stood there, looking like a fool, I expect, with my eyes bulging.

Odo jumped into the car and began throwing things out of it into my garden. Among other items I noticed a ham, a crate of bottles, and a salmon. 'Don't you worry about grub,' cried Odo. 'You're as bad as the Missis. When I told her last night we were going to stay with you she wanted me to send you a telegram, but of course I didn't. You might have refused to have us. Then she said you wouldn't have enough grub, and I said what about all that stuff she'd got stowed away in the storeroom, and she said that was for an emergency And I said this is an emergency. And as I'm a hearty eater we've brought plenty. These lobsters were swimming yesterday. Catch!'

I ignored the lobsters and advanced to greet the lady. She said, 'I ceased to apologise for Odo's behaviour very soon after I married him two years ago. The things he does and drags me into are beyond apologies. This unannounced descent upon you, for instance. He said you wouldn't mind because you and he were old friends. I do hope you are.' I said, 'We've known each other for twenty years and I've learned never to be surprised at anything he does. I'm very glad you've come.'

Mrs Odo gave a sigh of relief. 'Thank heavens for that,' she said. 'I mean … It's very kind of you to bear with us, but what I'm thanking heaven for is that you really are an old friend. You know, Odo's quite capable of planting me upon an entire stranger, so I've been spending most of the time during the drive here praying you really were an old friend and not merely a chance acquaintance.'

I said, 'Don't worry any more then. I'm very fond of that old madman of yours, and whatever he does is all right as far as I am concerned. He never told me he was married, but I congratulate him now. I don't know about congratulating you, though. I think you are either very brave or extremely rash. But do come in. We'll leave Odo to carry in the baggage. I don't suppose he told you why he suddenly decided to spend a week in this remote part of the world. He won't bother to tell me either, if I know him. Well, it doesn't really matter; but what I *do* want to know is, what on earth he's up to with that lifeboat? Has he any good reason for towing a lifeboat by road all across England, or is he just doing it for fun?'

'All I can tell you,' she replied, 'is that when he got home yesterday evening he asked me if I'd ever met you. I said I hadn't, and he said, "Well you soon will. We're going to stay with him for a week and we're starting tomorrow morning, because I'm testing the new boat at Farport."

Here Odo pranced in upon us. The man seldom walks. He is so full of supercharged energy that his usual mode of progression is at a trot, dancing upon his toes. He said, 'Ha! I told you you'd get on with Jim, Missis. I've dumped all the gear and grub in the hall. Where shall I put the boat?'

I said, 'I won't have it in the garden. Leave the thing in the lane, or run it into the next field.'

'Can't be done,' said Odo firmly. 'That boat's precious. More than rubies. *And* fragile. Got to be, you understand, for lightness. And she's bung-full of priceless gear. The wireless alone ... Why! there's over £300 of navigating instruments in her. Leave her in the road and the boys of the village will tear her to pieces. Put her in the field and the cows will eat her. Besides, she's a Number One, Air Ministry, Priority Secret. Prototype boat. For the Pacific. If the Ministry only knew I'd brought her by road, all this way, stark naked on a trailer ... Well, anyhow, I averaged thirty all the way and never stopped once, except for lunch and four or five times for beer, so nobody's had much chance to gaze at her. She'll have to go under lock and key here, though. Haven't you got a garage?'

I said, 'Yes. It's 20 feet long, and your boat's 30 at least. And it hasn't got a lock, anyway.'

'There's no building you can lock her up in this village,' I answered. 'All I can suggest is that you run

110

her back to Chemton – it's only about 16 miles – and see if the police can help you.'

Odo said, 'You're not trying, Jim. Where's all that noise coming from?'

'Airfield, just the other side of those trees,' I answered.

'Well, dash it!' cried Odo. 'Why didn't you tell me that at first? It's exactly what's wanted. Missis, we'll be back in twenty minutes. Make the tea. Jim, jump in the car and pilot me.'

I said, 'It's an American airfield, old chap, and they're very fussy. Won't let anyone near the place: I've tried to have a look at it several times, but they've posted M.P.s everywhere, all hung about with pistols and tommy-guns. I'm told they shoot to kill, too.'

Odo said, 'Pah! Come on. Get in! Don't be so faint-hearted.'

I got in. We drove off. I said, 'You'll never get into that airfield.'

Odo said, 'I will.'

I said, 'How?'

Odo said, 'Somehow.'

'Well, there's the M.P.,' I said. 'Just ahead, on the corner. And I'm going to switch off your ignition if you try to drive past him.'

The M.P. said, 'Halt! Show your pass, mister.'

Odo said, 'Sorry. I haven't got a pass.'

The M.P. said, 'Then you'll have to go back, brother.'

Odo said, 'I can't back with this trailer behind. And I can't turn round in this lane.'

The M.P. laughed. 'I guess you're right.' he said. 'You'll have to go ahead now. Straight ahead and out

111

by the main gate. Keep going and no monkeying around, mind! I'll phone through and warn 'em you're coming.'

We proceeded. Odo said, 'We're in.'

I said, 'Well, I'll be damned.'

Odo said, 'I'll bet that's headquarters, with the Stars and Stripes flying over it. We'll try it, anyway.'

He drew up in front of the building and went in. Presently he came out again, with a major, who shook hands with him and said, 'Well, good-bye, sir. Glad to have met you, Mr Hunter. That boat of yours sure looks bully. Drive her into the hangar and leave her there as long as you like. She'll be quite O.K. We keep a sentry on duty in that hangar, day and night.'

We left the lifeboat in the hangar and drove homewards. I said, 'How on earth did you do it?'

Odo said, 'Oh, just told him I wanted him to lock up a lifeboat for me. I think he thought I was drunk; but when he heard it was an Air-Sea Rescue lifeboat I'd designed specially for long distance work in the Pacific, he couldn't do enough for me. He said he guessed I'd save the lives of a whole lot of their boys out there. He guessed right. And here we are, home agin, and I told the missis we'd be back in twenty minutes and we are.'

Mrs Odo had made the tea and set it out in the garden all ready for us. She said, 'I made myself at home in your kitchen. I hope you don't mind.'

I said, 'It's very clever of you to do it, and I don't know how you found where everything was.'

Odo said, 'Yes, the Missis is clever. I've seen her do miracles.'

I said, 'Miracles! Then you're a good pair. I've just been watching him perform miracles, too, Mrs Odo.'

'I know,' she said. 'I mean, Odo never stops talking, as you know. But when he does stop and sits, laughing at himself, like that, then I know he's been up to something clever – or naughty. What have you done now, my pet?'

'Oh, nothing.' answered Odo. 'And I'm not laughing at myself. I'm laughing at Jim. He's just seen me do something quite simple and straight-forward, but, because he made up his mind beforehand it was going to be impossible, the old chump thinks I'm wonderful. And don't call her Mrs Odo any more, Jim. It sounds awful. Her name's Jane, but she answers best to Missis. Have some Gentleman's Relish on your toast, old sailor. I got hold of six dozen pots of it on D-Day plus One. Found some Americans drifting about in a broken-down landing barge and towed 'em in, and they gave me the stuff. As a mark of esteem and gratitude, they said, but really because they'd had nothing else to eat for thirty hours and they never wanted to see any more of it as long as they lived. Don't ask me where they got it. The thing that struck me was that after eating nothing else but this stuff, neat, for a day and a half, none of 'em were seasick. Have some more, Missis.'

'I will not,' said she. 'It's rather rich, but you've made it sound much too rich. Instead of talking nonsense, hadn't you better tell Jim precisely why you've dumped yourself, your wife, and your lifeboat upon him without any warning or apology?'

'Perfectly simple,' said Odo. 'I needed a holiday. What's more, I wanted a holiday. I haven't had one since the war began. I wanted a week's peace and quiet. And the boat was ready for testing. Also I was scheming to gain time, because I've another and better boat coming along. So I told the Ministry people I'd be ready to test this boat in a week's time, from Farport. They said, "Why now, and why Farport?" And I said, because I've got to have a week's absolute quiet and rest, and Farport was the nearest port to Jim's garden, which was the quietest, restfullest place I knew. So I proposed going there. So here we are. I'm going to sit here in the sun, and eat and sleep and do nothing for a whole week. I'll do nothing. Nothing at all. Except I've got to deliver the boat to the R.A.F. soon at their airfield near Farport, to let 'em fit her to her carrier aircraft, ready for the test drop. By the way, Jim, you're going to help me with the test drop.'

'Me!' I cried. 'Don't you believe it. I don't know what plan you've got in your horrid mind, but I do know I'm not going to let you drop me in a boat, out of an aircraft, into the cold North Sea. I'm too old for such games.'

'Nonsense,' replied Odo. 'All I want you to do is to let the Navy dump you in a rubber boat about 20 miles offshore. You'll represent a ditched bomber's crew. The rescue aircraft will fly out, and, when and if she finds you, she drops the lifeboat on parachutes and you get aboard and sail back to Farport. Nice little yachting trip for you. You'll enjoy it. Anyhow, you've got to come. I must have a man who can handle and sail a boat, and I'm absolutely relying on you. That's one reason I came here.'

I protested – hard. But, as I thought the thing over, it seemed to me it would be a very interesting operation to see. And Odo was relying on me, and we were old, tried shipmates. So I said I would do it, if I could wangle a day off duty from my chief in the Royal

Observer Corps.

Then the Missis said, 'Oh, Odo! What a shame.'

Odo said, 'Nonsense. It's yachting at the Government's expense. I knew he couldn't resist it.'

The Second Day of Odo's quiet and restful holiday began quietly. He announced that he would have his breakfast in bed, just to assure himself that he really was on holiday. He then slept solidly until tea-time. After tea he arose, a genius refreshed, and took the Missus and me to call on the American major at the airfield. The rest of the day was not quiet or restful.

If Americans like you they do not disguise the fact. They took to Odo immediately and completely. They took to the Missis, of course. And they even took to me. They gave us their airfield. They put us on the roof of the Control Tower, and dive-bombed us with a squadron of Mustangs. They took us up in a Flying Fort, just to see what my garden looked like from the air. They gave us quantities of something memorable, called 'Rye and Coke', in large glasses full of crushed ice. They gave us dinner, and I shall not forget the chicken á la Maryland, the corn on the cob, and the ice-cream made of cream. After dinner they sat us in saddle-back chairs in their movie-theatre, and showed us Hollywood's very latest colour film. They took us to the Mess and plied us with more crushed ice plus notable flavourings. We did not get home until two o'clock in the morning.

I said, 'Gosh! What a night. I thought you came here for peace and rest, Odo.'

Odo said, 'I did. And I'm getting 'em. I've had sixteen hours' sleep in the last twenty-four, and now I'm going to have seven more. Be realistic, Jim.'

The Third Day of Odo's peaceful holiday commenced at 9 a.m. when he arose, cooked breakfast, and brought me mine in bed. It is pleasant to awake to the smell of coffee and bacon. I said, 'This is very kind of you, Odo.'

He said, 'Not at all. I merely wanted to get you in a good temper this morning. I've got to deliver the boat to the R.A.F. today, and you've got to help me. The Missis has struck. She intends to sleep all day under your apple trees. You probably do, too, after last night. But you can't. It's your fault for living in a country that's all narrow lanes with right-angled corners. Towing a 30-foot trailer in these parts is a two-man job.'

We collected the boat from the hangar, eluded, with difficulty and tact, further American hospitalities, and set off on our 30-mile drive to Farport. In our first half-mile, at the bottom of a hill, at a corner, we met a traction-engine, towing a threshing-machine and a trailer full of coals. The lane was too narrow to allow us to pass, and neither outfit could go astern. I reviewed the deadlock, and decided at once it was a situation with which only a genius could cope. I sat back and lit my pipe. The driver of the tractor took much the same view as I did of the position. Said he, 'Somebody'll have to build a ruddy by-pass before we gets out of this mess.'

Odo said, 'We could uncouple the trailer and get a horse, if we knew where to get a horse, and tow it back up the hill and into the nearest field-gate. But that's going to take too long. I'll go back to the airfield and get the Yanks to lend us their crash outfit. I won't be long.'

He was not long. Neither were the Americans. I think it speaks well, both for Odo and our gallant Allies, that we were under way again in less than three-quarters of an hour. What is more, this time we proceeded with an American M.P. on a motor-cycle ahead of us, to keep our way clear. We gained the main road without further trouble, and here our escort left us, after presenting me with a packet of cigarettes and Odo with a packet of chewing-gum.

Odo drove on. Presently he said, 'Some people don't, but I like 'em.'

I said, 'What? Those chewing-gum things?'

Odo said, 'No, Americans.' He drove on at thirty knots. In due time we came to the RAF airfield, and drew up in front of the orderly-room. A Group Captain appeared. He looked at the boat and he looked at Odo, and he appeared to be perturbed. He said, 'D'you mean to tell me you've brought that boat all across England without any cover on her?'

Odo said, 'No, sir. I didn't mean to tell you, but now you've noticed it. I'll admit I brought her stark naked all the way.'

'Good gracious, man,' the Group Captain exclaimed. 'Don't you know that boat is a Number One Priority Secret?'

Odo said, 'No, she isn't, sir.'

The Group Captain said, 'But I tell you she is. I've had special instructions to that effect, direct from the Ministry. She's Most Secret, I tell you.'

'Don't you believe it,' said Odo. 'Since she left my yard she's been seen and admired by several hundred people. I left her in a public car park while I ate, and outside four or five pubs while I drank, and every time when I got back to her I found several score of people climbing all over her. So, whatever the Ministry says, I say she isn't secret.'

The G.C. said, 'You are Mr Hunter, I take it? Ah! They warned me not to be surprised at anything you might do. But I must say I'm surprised at what you have done. Would you mind telling me why you did it?'

'Willingly,' answered Odo. 'But, mind you, this is a secret. The Ministry don't know it yet, but I can tell you that the more the Jerries and the Japs know about this boat the better, because she's the only one of her type I'm going to turn out, and her successors are going to be quite different and much better.'

The G.C. grinned. 'Ho!' said he. 'That being the case, let's go to the Mess and see if they've got anything to drink there.'

The hospitality of the R.A.F. differs from that of the U.S. Army Air Force. The R.A.F. brand is less various but more persistent. Odo and I did not get back to our beds until 3 a.m.

The Fourth Day really was quiet. It was also restful, for me if not for Odo, because I had an inspiration and introduced him to a bow and some arrows. The potent witchery of archery then took complete possession of him, as I hoped it would. He shot at a target in the garden all day long, and he would have shot all night, too, if the light had not failed him.

On the Fifth Day, Odo's fingers were so sore from the friction of the bow-string that he could not draw his bow. He said, 'Oh! What a terrible pity! I've just discovered the most difficult and therefore the most enthralling sport there is and now, hang it! it's maimed me. What shall we do today?'

I said, 'Personally, I've got to get back to work. The Observer Corps gave me a week's holiday, but today's the end of it. I've got to go on duty now and I won't be back until the evening.'

Odo said, 'Then I'll come with you. I'd like to see what you Observer chaps are up to.'

I said, 'I'm afraid you can't. I work in the Ops. Room at the Chemston Centre. You talk about your Air Ministry Priority Secrets, but we really are secret. We keep ourselves locked up, with wardens on guard, and no one can get in or out without our special pass. The Corps doesn't like publicity. In fact, we hate it. Winston himself couldn't get into the Centre without a pass, so I'm afraid you can't either.'

Odo said, 'Ho! Very exclusive, aren't you? Then I'll amuse myself today. And, look here! How about the test-drop tomorrow? If you're on duty, you won't be able to come.'

I said I would ask my chief for a day off, and I trusted he would not give me one. I then fled.

At mid-day I was busy in the Ops. Room, helping to keep track of the hundreds of aircraft which were flying over our area, when I heard the stern voice of the Centre controller speaking through my ear-phones. It said, 'The commandant wishes to see you in his office immediately. The warden has caught a man breaking into the Centre through the canteen window, and the man says he's a friend of yours.'

I said, 'Oh, Lord! Odo!!'

The controller said, 'As you do appear to know the chap you'd better hurry. The police have already been sent for.'

I found the commandant seated at his desk, looking

outraged and very angry. In front of him stood Odo, looking naughty.

The commandant said, 'This person was caught in the act of breaking into the Centre. He has no pass, not even an Identity Card. He says he's a friend of yours.'

I said, 'I'm afraid he is, sir.'

'Then I will be glad,' the commandant said, 'if you can explain what he thinks he's doing, breaking in here like this. It's a serious business. I've sent for the police to deal with him. And, if you had anything to do with this, I warn you I shall take severe disciplinary action.'

Here Odo horrified me by remarking, 'Jim's responsible for the whole thing, commandant. He told me no one could possibly get in here without a pass, so I thought I'd show him how wrong he is. Also I wanted to see you to ask you to let Jim take tomorrow off, because, you see, I'm relying on him to help me bring in an airborne lifeboat the R.A.F. are dropping for me off Farport. I hope you will let him come, otherwise it will upset all the arrangements.'

The commandant gasped, 'What's this?' he cried. 'I have been warned by the R.A.F. about this lifeboat test. It's most secret. And here you come, breaking in here, and telling me all about it. Who are you?'

'Hunter's the name,' replied Odo. 'It's my lifeboat.'

'Good gracious!' the commandant exclaimed; 'are you Odo Hunter? I heard you were making these boats. Why didn't you say who he was at first, Jim. Very stupid of you. It would have saved all this – er – nonsense. I owned one of your yachts once, Mr Hunter. The *Vixen*, in 1925. I won, or rather *she* won all the local races that season. She was a real little beauty, and I'm very glad to meet her designer. Now, let's see. Sit

120

down, Mr Hunter, do. And you, Jim, run along. Get back to the job. And tell the warden we shan't need the police after all.'

I did as I was bid and returned to my work in the Ops. Room.

Presently I observed Odo entering our Holy of Holies. He was escorted by no less a person than the commandant, who showed him everything. All Odo said to me was, 'Passes, my foot!'

When I got home Odo said, 'You nearly lost your job today, my son.'

I said, 'Yes. Thanks to your nonsense, you old maniac.'

But Odo said, 'No. Thanks to me, you've kept it. Your boss took me out to lunch, and he said he wouldn't give you tomorrow off, so I'd better let him go instead of you. However, I resisted his artfulness, and he's letting you go. Told me to tell you so. Aren't you pleased with me for arranging it so nicely?'

We started for Farport at five o'clock next morning. When we were 15 miles from anywhere Odo said, 'You'd better take off your coat and tie and hide 'em in the back of the car before we get to Farport. You'll find a dirty old fisherman's pullover in my bag. Put that on.'

I said, 'What for?'

Odo said, 'Because you're my bos'n, and you've got to look like a bos'n. I have to keep on telling you this is Most Secret. If the Navy or the R.A.F. find out you're a mere civilian, butting in on this, they'll probably shoot you.'

I said, 'Hang it, Odo, I don't know that I like this.'

Odo laughed and accelerated. 'You can't back out

now,' said he. 'And Farport's a naval base these days. All barbed wire and sentries. I'll get you in all right on my over-all pass as my bos'n, but when we are in you'd better begin calling me "Sir" and "Mr Hunter". There'll be all sorts of Ministry V.I.P.s coming out with us in the destroyer, so you'd better act your part properly and no nonsense. Carry my bag when we go aboard, and all that.'

There was no getting out of it now for me. I could not even get out of the car. Odo saw to that. He drove at 50 miles an hour and skidded round all corners. So I said, 'Very good, sir. Mr Hunter, you're a kidnapping, double-crossing, old scoundrel.'

We reached the quay at Farport at 06.10 hours, and found a destroyer, a naval Commander, two Wing-Commanders, and several important-looking civilians awaiting us.

The Commander said, 'Good morning, Mr Hunter. You're ten minutes late so we'd better get aboard at once and get cracking.'

Odo said, 'Right, sir. I'm sorry I'm late. Bos'n, where's my bag?'

'I've got it, Mr Hunter,' I said, 'Leave it to me, sir.'

'Hullo!' exclaimed the Commander, staring hard at me. 'What are you doing here?'

I said, 'Oh, lawks!'

Odo slapped his leg and burst out laughing. 'Rumbled!' said he. 'I might have known you can't slip anything past the Navy.'

The Commander said, 'We met at Plymouth, after the last Fastnet race, if you remember. I'm glad to meet you again, but-what are you doing here? I've got to know, I'm afraid.'

'When in trouble, tell the truth,' said Odo. 'I've given my regular bos'n a holiday, Commander. And I asked Jim here to take his place for the job. He's got no official permit, but you know him and I know him. Also, if you don't let him come, this test drop doesn't come off, because I'm not going without Jim. What about it?'

I could see the Commander thinking things over, even though it took him only a tenth of a second to decide. 'Oh, come aboard,' said he. 'It's highly irregular, but I'll take the responsibility. Let's go.'

Highly irregular? Maybe. But God bless the Royal Navy, I say.

It does get things done.

I said, 'Thank you, Commander. And from now on, Odo, you can carry your own damned bag.'

Our destroyer fled out of the harbour and proceeded eastwards at the rate of knots.

'The North Sea, or German Ocean,' remarked Odo, looking at the brown water flecked with white wave-tops. 'When you and I get aboard our little rubber raft, old shipmate, we're going to get wet.'

'How far out are we going?' I asked.

'About 20 miles,' Odo answered. 'We've got to get out of sight of land, because these Ministry blokes are very jealous and they don't want anyone else to see what's going on. Now, let's go and scrounge some breakfast, for heaven knows when we shall next taste grub.'

At 7.20 our ship went full speed astern and stopped. Two seamen dropped a rubber raft overboard and held it there while Odo and I climbed in. They handed us two smoke-floats and a camera in a rubber bag. One

Wing-Commander said, 'Don't make smoke until you identify the rescue aircraft.' The other Wing-Commander said, 'Take a photo of the dummy before you touch anything.' And the Commander said, 'Good luck, chaps. Hold Tight! We're off.' At 7.25 the destroyer was steaming full speed away from us, and soon grew small on the horizon.

Odo said, 'Nice work.'

I said, 'What's he rushing off like that for and leaving us here all alone?'

'U-boats,' answered Odo. 'It isn't healthy to keep a ship stopped in these waters very long.'

I said, 'Gosh! I'm beginning to feel lonely. I hadn't thought of U-boats. And what about hostile aircraft?'

'That's why the Wing-Commander told us not to make smoke until we were sure,' Odo answered.

'I wish I'd stayed at home,' I said. 'I like this job less and less the more I have to do with it. I'm sitting in the wet and I think I'm going to be seasick. In all my life I've never even *felt* seasick, but there's something so horrid and leery about the movements of this dreadful raft that I do believe I'm going to spoil my record.'

'Same here,' said Odo through clenched teeth. 'It's not the pitching or the rolling, but the creepy-crawly way the bottom of this thing heaves and bulges and sinks *under* you that ...'

I said, 'Shut up! Don't talk about it.'

Here Odo dived overboard. Presently he reappeared and hung on to the side of the raft. 'That's better,' said he. 'Being in that raft felt like sitting on a lot of soft, undulating blondes. Horrible. In another two seconds I'd have lost my breakfast.'

I clenched my teeth on my breakfast and managed

to keep it with me. 'When,' I asked, 'are we due to be rescued?'

'Eight o'clock,' answered Odo. 'What time is it now?'

'7.55-and I hear an aircraft,' I said.

'Chuck a smoke-float overboard then,' said Odo. 'Let's get cracking. I'm getting cold.'

I said, 'Wait a bit. I can see it now to the east of us. A black, twin-engined machine, at about a thousand feet. Odo, I don't like the look of him. He may be hostile, coming in from the eastward like this.'

'I thought you told me you Observer Corps chaps could identify any aircraft as soon as you heard it,' Odo remarked.

'So we can,' I said, 'provided we've seen or heard a similar aircraft before. But I've never seen or heard anything like this one. It's coming straight for us and losing height. It's rather like a Wellington, but it's too big. And where's the lifeboat anyway? I can't see it about her anywhere. I think we'd better stand-by to duck.'

'You wouldn't see the lifeboat,' said Odo. 'It's designed w make a snug fit under the Warwick's underbody.'

'Of course!' I cried, for I was much relieved. 'A Warwick. I've not seen one before, but that's what it is.' I set off a smoke-float. The Warwick circled twice and then headed for us at less than a thousand feet, dead up wind. And then a series of miracles happened, or so it seemed to me. The bottom of the aircraft fell off and hurtled down, straight at us. I prepared to dive overboard, but I stayed where I was when three enormous parachutes materialized above the falling

125

object. Three rockets then shot out of the thing, trailing bright yellow ropes. 'Sea anchor and two life-lines,' said Odo. 'Isn't it lovely. All going like clockwork. Now watch the self-righting chambers grow on each end of her. It's rubber and compressed air doing that.'

I saw the boat take on, in mid-air, the characteristic shape of a lifeboat with its short lengths of high, cambered deck at bow and stern. Then the boat hit the water within 20 yards of the raft, the parachutes detached themselves, and I became enveloped in acres of clinging silk fabric and several miles of cord. Odo was already aboard the lifeboat when I emerged from my canopy.

'Well done,' said he. 'You've saved two 'chutes. Try and grab the other one. It's just going under water on your starboard beam.'

I said, 'I've got all the parachutes I need.'

Odo said, 'All right. Let it go then. It only cost a couple of hundred pounds; and you're a taxpayer.'

I retrieved the third parachute and paddled my raft alongside the lifeboat. I climbed aboard. Odo was taking photographs of a dummy man who lay strapped on the bottom amidships. I saw a heavy steel hook sticking into the thing's head.

'Makes me feel thoughtful,' said Odo, shaking the dummy heartily by its limp hand. 'I wanted to be dropped in this boat instead of the dummy, but the R.A.F. wouldn't let me. Said they preferred to try it with a dummy first and see what happened. Well, this is what happened. I called them a lot of cissies. Said we were fighting a war, not running a girls' school. But I couldn't shake 'em. Am I glad, now? That parachute release hook dropped 20 feet and weighs 20 pounds. I shall have to apologise to those Wing Commanders.'

Odo began to shiver. 'Burrr!' he said, 'I'm cold. Let's go. In the bottom aft you'll see an armoured-glass porthole. Look through it and tell me if there's anything foul of our propeller.' 'All clear,' I said.

Odo pressed a button and our motor immediately sprang to life.

Odo said, 'Lovely. Ship the tiller, Jim, and take her home. We're 20 miles east, true, from Farport. The compass is let into the deck under your feet. Work out the course to steer. There's a deviation table, charts, ruler, pencils, and everything else you want in that locker marked "Navigator". Let me know if the pencils are sharpened. They ought to be. Now, you do the work. I'm going to get myself warm and comfortable. The rum ought to be in the "Medical Stores" locker. It is. And flocks of chemical hot-water bottles. Just what the doc. ordered. And here's what I'm looking for. Waterproof, eiderdown sleeping-bag, complete with hood and zip-fastener. I'll zip myself in here with six hot-water bottles and the rum, and be as right as rain. Have an Energizing Tablet? No. Well what else have we? Tinned grub and fishing-lines; cans of fresh water and chemical distilling gadget. Barley sugar, malted milk tablets, chocolates, cigarettes, programmes, No. This is the "Instruction Book". "How to sail to windward" in three paragraphs. I wrote most of this book myself, and it's hot. Any ditched aircrew that's lucky enough to get one of these boats dropped to 'em is in clover – if only they'll read the Instruction Book first. Have some more rum. If I wasn't so snug and warm in this bag I'd rig up the wireless and send a telegram to the Missis, saying we'll be home to tea. Can you see the land yet?'

I said, 'No. Only thing in sight is the destroyer, and she's hull down ahead of us, hurrying those Ministry blokes home to lunch, I guess. How much petrol have we got?'

'Six hundred miles of it,' Odo answered. 'Enough to get home from the middle of the North Sea or the Bay, but useless in the Pacific, where you may get ditched a thousand miles from home. That's why I designed this boat *to sail*. She's got two masts, a jib, mainsail and mizzen, a dagger centre-board plate, and a drop rudder. What she is really is a big, unsinkable, fast racing canoe. Now, there's a nice breeze, and I never did like motor-boating. Let's sail.'

With the help of the Instruction Book (Odo refused to help), I stepped and stayed the masts in no time, dropped the centre-board and rudder, and made sail. Thereafter I enjoyed three hours of real yachting and Odo went to sleep. The boat went faster under sail than with her motor running, and by the time we had reached the entrance to Farport Harbour I had come to the conclusion that any crashed aircrew could, in a similar boat, get themselves safely to land from the middle of the Pacific without much hardship. Indeed, with luck and if anyone aboard knew how to sail a boat, the job of surviving could be turned into a pleasantish yachting cruise.

I woke up Odo and told him so. He said, 'Yes, I know. The boat's all right, but don't forget-we killed the dummy. And until I can drop a man in an airborne lifeboat without killing him I'll never be satisfied. It's got to be done, you know.'

I said, 'All right, so long as you don't try any more

128

of your games and think you're going to drop me. I'm too old and much too scared. Well, there's our destroyer, tied up to the quay. What do we do now?'

'Berth alongside her,' answered Odo. 'And if anyone asks you what you think of this boat, you say she isn't up to her job. Remember the dummy. Also I have good reasons.'

I berthed as directed, and we handed the boat over to the Wing Commanders. They seemed pleased. Said one, 'The flight and drop tests were one hundred per cent perfect. How did your end go?'

'Recovery, motor, sailing, and equipment one hundred per cent,' Odo answered, handing over the camera; 'but when you've had a look at these photos you'll know we'll never drop a man in this type of boat without killing him. The dummy's head was stove in, and the landing shock would break a man's back. And it would have been my head and my back if you hadn't got more sense than I have. Thanks for saving my life. Now I've got to go ahead and devise some completely protective structure and equipment for the man who's dropped – and there isn't room for anything like that in this type.'

'Afraid we can't wait for any new design,' said the senior Ministry official. 'These boats are needed in quantity immediately. The war in the Pacific is warming up fast and it's a case of save time, save lives. This boat has now passed all tests, and I'm going to recommend the Ministry to put the type into full production at once.'

'You'll save time and lose lives that way,' Odo answered. 'Give me a month at most, and I'll give you a boat that'll save more lives than this one ever will.'

'This one has passed her tests one hundred per cent and that's good enough for anybody,' said the official. '"The best is the enemy of the good", Mr Hunter, and we can't throw away a whole month. That's quite impossible.'

'Very well, then,' said Odo, 'I'll have to see if I can do the impossible. Good-bye everybody. I'm going home to tea.'

During our drive home I said, 'I don't get the point in your argument with that Ministry chap, ado. Haven't you and I proved today that the boat is ideal for the job of rescuing a ditched crew, even though a man *wasn't* dropped in her? I think the chap was right in his decision.'

Odo said, 'If you had a few more brains, Jim, you'd be half-witted. You ought to get a job in the Ministry. It's difficult to make chaps like you *see*. But I'll try. Listen! What was proved today was that an airborne lifeboat can be dropped, on a fine day in a moderate wind and sea, close enough to the target to enable two fit, strong able seamen to get aboard her and· sail her home. What was *not* proved is that the boat can be dropped in a gale of wind and a rough sea close enough to a rubber raft to enable the raft's crew of cold, wet, starved, exhausted airmen to get themselves aboard the lifeboat. The odds are, in such conditions they'd never manage. The lifeboat would blow away from them before they could get near it. As for sailing her home, if they did manage to get aboard, the odds are none of the men would know how to sail a boat, and they'd never get anywhere. That's why we've got to drop a man in the lifeboat who knows all about it. He would clear away the parachute gear, start the motor, pick up the airmen, and show them how to sail home. That's why I want them to give me time to devise something in my new boat that'll keep the man who's dropped in the boat alive. That will save many more lives in the long-run than will ever be lost in one month through lack of boats. I know it, but no one else seems to see it. All those lives to be lost just because someone wants to save time. The stupidity of man! It's terrible, terrible.'

After that outburst, Odo was silent for a long time. This is something which never happens to him unless he is asleep — or concentrating on a problem. He was certainly not concentrating on his driving; for the car wandered all across the road, narrowly missed two lorries and a cyclist, and went right-handed round a traffic roundabout.

I said, 'For heaven's sake come out of your trance, Odo, or let me drive.'

Then Odo brought the car to a screaming standstill. He smote the steering-wheel with his clenched fists and cried out, 'By God! I've got it.'

I said, 'Got what?'

He said, 'I've got the idea. I've got it. But have I got the time? I see how to give a man protection in the new boat so that the drop won't kill him. But it means a change in design. The construction will be a bit tricky. The details want working out, and that'll take time. And I haven't any time. In two or three days at the most I'll get the Ministry's orders to go ahead, full blast, with the production of the type we tested· today. And when the Ministry does make a decision like that it's practically impossible to change it. The only thing I can do is to get in ahead of them. I've got to confront them with the new type boat, complete and ready for testing before they make their decision. And that means I've got to get on with it in the very devil of a hurry.'

He then started the car with a jerk, and began to drive furiously.

'Not a second to lose,' said he presently. 'Jim, I've got to get back to my drawing-office tonight. I'll pick up the Missis and our gear and drive home, non-stop. With luck I'll get to work by midnight. Sorry to leave you like this. But you understand. This job's *urgent*.'

We drew up at my house to the screaming of brakes and clamorous horn blowings. Odo dashed out, roaring, "Missis, Missis! Pack up, quick. Now. At once. Got to get home tonight. There's a hell of an urgent job on. Quick, Missis, quick. Hurry. Let's get going.'

The Missis, I must say, reacted most nobly to this unexpected trumpet-call to action. She arose from her deck-chair under the apple trees without any expostulation or argument, and got cracking. She was used to Odo's ways, of course, but, still, I had to marvel at her. She did not waste time packing. She brought out a double armful of clothes and gear, and dumped them in the back of the car. Odo followed with the suitcases, and threw them in on top of everything. He said, 'Good-bye, Jim. Sorry about this, but, anyway, we did have a nice, quiet holiday while it lasted.'

I said, 'Good-bye, Missis. Good-bye, Odo. It's been lovely having you.' I would have said more, but I did not get the chance, because Odo let in his clutch with a bang and departed at speed, blowing his horn and waving his arm out of the window.

I said, 'Well, well, well,' and made myself a nice hot cup of tea. I needed it.

The house seemed very quiet.

Send Down a Dove

Charles MacHardy

IT WAS EARLY MORNING. As the first, dim diffusion of light edged the rim of the eastern horizon the submarine crept towards the entrance to the Skagerrak. To port lay Naze Point; a faint smudge in the surrounding gloom. The wind had died to a light breeze. A long swell, cold, grey and menacing, rolled out from the Baltic and into the North Sea, lifting the bows of the submarine with a gentle, drawn-out swish.

The only other sounds that disturbed the quiet of early dawn were the deep throbbing note of the diesels and the wild, rising cry of the gulls, as they circled near land. It was as if they were sounding an alarm at the presence of the intruder.

Lieutenant Robinson, who had the watch on deck, shivered in the coldness of the dawn as he reached with stiff fingers to draw the collar of his duffel coat more tightly round his neck. His nose and cheekbones felt like bits of ice stuck to his face, but, with no wind to penetrate his clothing, his body was reasonably warm. Stamping his feet, as the cold bit into his toes, he glanced round at the two look-outs. The grey, shapeless figures might have been carved from stone. Robinson carefully wiped the lens of his night-glasses and returned to scan his own sector of the horizon.

Since coming on watch a mood of excitement had steadily grown within him, little nervous tremors shooting down his spine. The feeling, though aroused by fear, was not unpleasant. In fact Robinson's fears were acting as a stimulant as he tasted the sour-sweet essence of approaching danger. In just a few hours they would be in the Skagerrak and could expect to meet enemy forces. It was a prospect that thrilled the lieutenant and tingled his nerve endings with an electric charge that gave pleasure at the same time as it hurt.

He scanned the dark water ahead. Only a few hours now. But first they had to get through the minefield that barred their path like a giant booby trap. The thought of the deadly, invisible canisters of explosives sent fresh galvanic surges of energy through his nerves; but this time the feeling was entirely unpleasant and offered no thrills. Robinson tried to shut the thought off but it kept returning, like a twinge of toothache, to disturb his mood of swashbuckling gallantry.

He glanced at his watch, screwing his eyes up as he tried to make out the position of the hands on the faintly glowing luminous dial. 0540 hours. Time to call the captain. He bent down and cupped a hand over the voice-pipe.

A few minutes later Cheney arrived on the bridge. He wore no coat but he'd wrapped a heavy towel round his neck, tucking the ends into his jacket.

He grunted sourly to Robinson and moving over to the far side of the bridge, craned his head upwards to look at the overhanging cloud. For a long minute he inspected the sky, sniffing about like a dog trying to pick up a scent, as he read the weather signs. He turned to Robinson.

'We'll go to diving stations in ten minutes,' he said in a low growling voice. Without waiting for a reply he crossed over to the hatch and clambered back down the conning-tower ladder. In the control-room he went immediately across to the chart table and with a quick, decisive movement whipped back the canvas cover. Five minutes later, Brangwyn, having been called by the control-room messenger, arrived, rubbing his eyes and working his mouth open and shut as if he'd swallowed something unpleasant. He hung around for a few minutes, pacing about and rubbing his shoulders, before he picked up the Tannoy and announced diving stations. Within seconds of his replacing the speaker the crew began to filter into the control-room, grumbling amongst themselves in low tones as they shivered in the early morning cold.

Cheney, in the corner, seemed oblivious of everything as he studied the chart with deep concentration. His whole attention was absorbed by the warning red cross-hatched marks that indicated the position of the minefield. He stroked his chin thoughtfully. Slack water would be in about an hour. After that they would have the advantage of the flooding tide. By his calculations they would enter the minefield at 0900 hours. Three hours to go; He drew back the cover on the chart.

'All right, Number One ... we'll dive now, stand by,' he said, crossing the control-room and pausing for an instant with his foot on the bottom rung of the ladder before he made his way up top again. A few seconds later Robinson and the two look-outs came clattering down the conning-tower as the klaxon squawked out its warning cry. Echoing down from the top of the tower there came the dull sound of the upper-hatch slamming shut.

Before the first light of dawn the submarine had slipped quietly beneath the waves and buried herself in the depths.

Levelling off at 100 feet Brangwyn caught a trim. The hands fell out of diving stations and crept quietly back to their sleeping quarters, tip-toeing their way forward in the sudden silence that had fallen with the stopping of the diesels when they'd dived. It was as if they were fearful of making the slightest noise now that they were approaching the minefield. They turned in but few of them slept. Though the day had only begun they longed deeply for the night to fall, when they would surface free of the terrors of the mined channel ahead.

Breakfast would be ready in a couple of hours but no one had any appetite for food.

Cheney stood by the chart table sipping a cup of hot coffee which the steward, Cadbury, had brought him. Since the first light Cheney had been keeping a periscope watch in between frequent visits to the chart. The time was 0845. Cheney drained his coffee in one gulp, had one last look at the chart and crossed over to the big for'ard periscope. A dozen pairs of eyes followed him.

'Up periscope.'

Silence gripped the men in the control-room as the periscope hissed out of the well.

Cheney snapped the handles open from a squatting

position, unflexing his legs as it rose. He nestled his forehead firmly into the contours of the moulded rubber eyepiece. 'Hold it.'

The long column slid to a halt. Cheney began a circling movement with his feet as he swung the periscope through an arc, scanning the horizon. He took a deep breath and straightened up, knuckling his eyes for a second before he bent forward again and repeated the procedure.

The side-stepping motion of his feet slowed and finally stopped. For a long time he remained motionless, breathing audibly.

Clack, clack. The handles snapped back into the periscope housing. Cheney straightened up as the periscope slid away down into the well.

'All right, Number One. We'll go to diving stations now. Shut all bulkhead doors and ventilation trunking. Shut off for depth charging.'

They had arrived at the minefield.

'Diving stations ... diving stations ... diving stations.' Brangwyn's voice, distorted by the Tannoy, rang out through the submarine. The echoes had scarcely died when the first members of the crew came lurching and bleary-eyed into the control-room.

Cheney waited till Brangwyn had reported all hands closed up. He walked over to the Tannoy and unhooked it from its bracket. Holding the speaker up to his mouth he cleared his throat once or twice before pressing the contact button.

'Hallo, hallo. This is the Captain speaking. We are now about to go through the minefield. During passage we will remain at diving stations and the boat will be shut-off for depth charge routine. Only under exceptional circumstances will the bulkhead doors be opened. They will be opened of course to allow meals to be served ... The coxswain has arranged that Leading Cook Donahue will supply tea and sandwiches. These will be served by the P.O.'s messman and the wardroom steward at intervals during the day. This will be the only occasion I will permit the opening of bulkhead doors ... except in emergency. You all understand? Good. I needn't remind you we are quite close to the coast of occupied territory and you will go about your duties as quietly as you can.

'It is known that Jerry has a number of listening posts in. the area ...' The Tannoy crackled and the voice broke up into meaningless sounds. It was some seconds before he was heard again ... 'you will be very careful not to drop anything. Go about your duties as quietly as you can. We don't want Jerry nosing around on top of us.' The voice paused for a few seconds and then, as everyone waited expectantly, 'It will probably be early evening before we're clear of the minefield ... when we surface I want everyone to be on their toes. We can expect to get some attention from enemy anti-submarine aircraft patrols ... that is all.' The voice broke off abruptly.

Slowly and methodically, following the captain's address, the crew began shutting off the boat for depth charge routine, cutting off the ventilation trunking and swinging the heavy bulkhead doors shut, finally knocking on the dog clips. Within a few minutes they had sealed the submarine off into separate compartments. The only link now was by means of the telephone exchange. Their job done, with nothing else to do but wait and hope now, the men sat down and began nursing their private claustrophobic fears.

In the fore-ends C.P.O. Wells had just finished checking the dog-clips on the rear watertight door. He was going forward to check the door dividing the compartment from the tube-space, when from somewhere above his head he heard a faint voice hailing him. He looked up towards the deckhead. Mitchell, the sick seaman, was leaning out over the edge of his hammock. He didn't look well and his skin had a strange colour.'

'What's up then, Mitch?' Wells asked. 'Feeling a bit groggy?'

'What's going on, Chief?' The voice lacked strength. 'What are you shutting the bulkhead doors for? Have they spotted something up top?'

Wells reached up an arm and patted Mitchell on the shoulder. 'Take it easy, Mitch. Nothing's happening. Nothing to get worried about ... just routine that's all.' Mitchell must have been sleeping when the captain was on the Tannoy, Wells realised.

'We haven't been spotted or anything ...?'

'I told you. Stop worrying. Nobody's seen anything.'

'But the doors ...?

Wells inspected the thin pallid face peering over the edge of the canvas. There was no point in trying to deceive the bloke. After all it wasn't his first patrol in submarines.

'Well, the skipper thinks there might be some mines about.'

'Mines?' Mitchell made the word sound a dread disease.

His mouth worked for a moment and then he

leaned back in his hammock. Wells could no longer see him but he could hear him.

'I wish somebody would tell me what's going on. What are we supposed to be doing? Are we at Norway yet?'

Even though Mitchell's face was hidden Wells forced his own features into a grin. 'Listen, mate, I'm only the T.G.M. – remember? If you want to find out the answers to those questions you'd better nip along to the control-room and ask the skipper. If you catch him in a good mood he might even tell you. Now get your head down and get some sleep and forget about it.'

Wells slipped under the hammocks beckoning to Mulholland as he went forward. The tall lanky figure got up from the locker. Wells took his arm.

'Just keep your eye on Mitch, Scouse,' he said in a low whisper. 'I think he's feeling a bit dicky and … well, just keep an eye on him.'

Mulholland sneaked a glance at Mitchell's hammock. 'Right, Chief. I'll do that. What was he on about just now, anyway?'

'He wasn't on about anything. Just keep your eye on him, that's all I want you to do.'

Mulholland shrugged and looked round at the sealed-off compartment. 'Well, he's not likely to go any place.'

'Neither are you, or me for that matter, but I'm making it your responsibility, you long bugger. Okay?'

Mulholland spread his hands. 'All right, Chief. Anything for peace and quiet.' He turned lazily on his heel and made his way back to the locker. Leaning forward on the table he pillowed his head on his folded arms and closed his eyes.

Wells said nothing, he knew Mulholland wasn't asleep and the slightest alien sound would have him up on his feet as alert as a cat. It was just a habit that Mulholland had, this trick of closing his eyes at odd moments. He never suspected that it might get him into serious trouble one day.

Barbour, another member of Wells's three-man torpedo crew was stretched out on the other locker gazing vacantly up at the deckhead.

'What was all that about, Scouse?' he muttered from the corner of his mouth.

'The chief was asking me to tally up the hours you spend lying on your back. He thinks it might be a record,' Mulholland answered without bothering to open his eyes.

'Yaaagh,' Barbour made a sound of deep disgust. 'Go and get knotted.'

'You shouldn't speak disrespectfully to senior ratings or you might find yourself painting out the bilges when we get back,' Mulholland mumbled in a tired voice.

'Yeh, when we get back. I'll worry about it then.'

Kennedy, the third member of the T.G.M.'s team of three torpedo-men and the youngest member of the ship's company, heard the brief exchange between Mulholland and Barbour but he was too engrossed to pay much attention to it. He was too busy playing the role of faithful dog to the T.G.M. to bother about anything else. For Kennedy had a sort of hero-worship feeling for the T.G.M. and trotted round at his heels hanging on every word and faithfully carrying out each instruction. Perhaps his attitude wasn't all that surprising ... Kennedy's father had died long before he had the chance to get to know him. Childhood had been an unfortunate and unhappy affair. A time when not only did he lose his father but also both his brothers. One had died in infancy and the other at the age of nine; the infant from pneumonia and the elder from diphtheria. This combination of losses was far too great a mystery for a five-year-old to even begin to comprehend and he was glad to accept his mother's explanation that they had all departed from earth to a place where they would be safe and happy.

The Kennedys had been farm workers and lived in a small house some miles away from the nearest village. At school young Kennedy was able to laugh and play with the other children, but he would fall into unnaturally silent brooding moods on his return to a home from which all the warmth and vitality seemed to have fled.

Fortunately, being born of peasant stock, he'd inherited an ability to survive, along with a kind of stoical, Calvinistic independence of mind. But though this helped, the absence of a central, dominating theme in his life, caused by the death of his father, was something he was to feel throughout his childhood and early teens. It was no surprise, therefore, that when he found himself plunged into a new environment the rugged, masculine figure of the T.G.M. with his almost God-like authority became the focal point of Kennedy's thwarted emotions. For the first time in his life he had a hero he could worship.

Wells had finished inspecting the dog-clips on the bulkhead door. He stepped back, adjusting the angle of his cap and frowning slightly.

Kennedy had put the clips on the door. 'Is it okay,

Chief?' he asked anxiously.

Wells started, he'd been thinking what a fat lot of good the door would be if they hit a mine. He gave a short dry laugh and struck the vault-like door with the edge of his fist. 'It'd better be, laddie. There's an awful lot of water out there.'

The youthful skin on Kennedy's forehead furrowed. 'What's it like, Chief? The ... the ...?' He hesitated as if frightened to put his thoughts into words.

'What's it like? Bloody cold, son. And wet.'

'No, not that. I don't mean the water,' he grinned sheepishly, 'I mean the ... the minefield. W-what's it like?'

The T.G.M. folded his arms and shook his head. 'Of all the daft bloody questions. You've seen a mine haven't you?' Kennedy nodded dumbly.

'Well, that's what it's like then, only a lot more of them and all stuck in the hoggin' like coconuts waiting for some daft bastard to have a go.'

Kennedy looked a bit hurt at this. He'd hoped to get a serious answer to his question. Wells misinterpreted the look. 'Don't let it get you down, son,' he slapped Kennedy on the back. 'We've been through a lot worse than this. Don't worry. Just leave it to the skipper, we'll get through all right.' Kennedy opened his mouth to put the question again but Wells held a warning finger up to his lips, at the same time jerking his thumb in the direction of Mitchell's hammock. 'Keep it down'

A tinge of colour crept to Kennedy's cheeks. 'Sorry, Chief,' he whispered.

Wells held up his hand. 'Okay, forget it. Now follow me.' Mulholland looked up from the table at the

T.G.M.'s approach.

'We're going to be a long time closed up, Scouse. A couple of you might as well get your heads down and grab some sleep. Kennedy here and Barbour can have the first go. All right?'

'Great idea, Chief. Just like Aggie Weston's, eh? Will you make us a cup of tea, an' all,' Mulholland cracked.

'Listen, you long, Liverpool bastard, I'll have you polishing the brasswork.'

Barbour, already half-way into his hammock, stopped and grinned. 'That's right, Chief. It'll do him good.'

Mulholland's answer was to yawn and straighten up from the table. 'One of these days I'm going to go on strike.' He screwed up his eyes painfully. 'I suppose those two goons had better have the first go. They'd be just as well with their heads down for all the good they are. Well, what are you waiting for, kidder? You heard what the Chief said or do you want to stay and polish the brasswork? He wasn't kidding, you know.'

Kennedy stepped forward eagerly. 'I don't mind staying up, Scouse, if you want to turn in first.' Mulholland looked at the T.G.M.

'Suit yourselves,' said Wells.

'Okay, kidder,' Mulholland pulled himself to his feet. 'There's one thing about it, my old mum said I'd never die in bed, so you're all right for a bit.' He climbed up on to the table and hoisted himself into his hammock.

Wells turned to Kennedy. 'Don't mind that dismal bastard. He's always dripping about something or other.'

'A Jeremiah,' Kennedy smiled.

'Eh?' Wells frowned suspiciously.

'That's what Jock Bain says: a Jeremiah. You know, from the Bible?'

'Oh? Well, right then, me lad, Jeremiah or no Jeremiah the bastard was right about one thing,' Wells said, swinging round to survey the compartment, 'you *are* going to polish the brasswork. Just look at the state of the place. It's like a broker's shop.' He crossed over towards the rear door. 'Take a look at this lot, it's covered in shit.' He pointed to the copper urn. 'It's a wonder you don't all have Gyppo gut, drinking out of that lot.'

Kennedy followed him cautiously, not very sure whether he was being kidded or not. He'd never heard of anyone polishing brasswork on patrol before.

'Just look at that mess.' Wells's finger stabbed the air. Kennedy looked. The urn had long since lost its metallic sheen and was covered in dark brown stains and thick patches of dull green. The brass tap dripped steadily, the drip tray overflowing and spilling its contents on the slopping deck.

Wells pushed his cap back on his head, 'Get a kettle,' he said. 'Go on. Chop chop. Get a kettle, I said.' The T.G.M. was determined that he would keep the young seaman busy so as he wouldn't have a chance to brood or think about the barrier of mines that surrounded them.

Kennedy came back with the kettle. 'Okay. Now when you've emptied the copper I want you to clean it so's I'll be able to see my face in it. I'll strip that tap out and fix it for once and all. The bloody thing drips every patrol. Let's get cracking then.'

A few minutes later the copper was emptied. Kennedy laid it down on its side on a tea chest and literally covered it in Brasso. He rubbed away furiously as the T.G.M. fitted a new washer to the tap. If it took him the rest of the day he was going to get the urn shining like a mirror. Absorbed in his task completely, Kennedy forgot all about where they were – and where they were heading –for the moment.

The control-room was as quiet as a grave. The air hung heavy. It was like the still, hushed period before the outbreak of a thunder-storm. Except for the helmsman and the two planesmen, who had a job to do, the rest of the crew stood around, changing position only when their limbs began to ache and cramp up. Solemn-faced and silent they resembled a group of pall bearers waiting for the coffin to arrive.

Titt leant against the for'ard watertight door and licked his dry lips. Since they had gone to diving stations and the heavy door clanged shut behind him he had been staring fixedly at the foreplane's depth gauge; not really seeing anything but just gazing abstractedly at the soft green light that spilled over the giant dial. In other circumstances the light might have had a soothing effect but now it had an ominous quality, like some fearful phosphorescent glow in a damp, subterranean cavern. It reminded him of a film he'd seen as a boy. The film had been about a group of miners trapped in a pitfall and to create a heightened effect the whole sequence had been shot in monochrome red. The result had been awesome and terrifying.

Titt shifted his gaze to where the captain was standing in the centre of the control-room.

Cheney was standing by the for'ard periscope, his shoulders hunched and his body inclined forward slightly in an attitude of deep concentration. Now and then the whites of the eyes would glint briefly in the dim light as he raised his head to look over the helmsman's shoulder at the gyro compass. Apart from this slight movement Cheney remained as still as the others.

Titt became conscious of the gradual tightening of his chest muscles. Though his mind was well under control his body had reacted independently to the tension induced by their arrival at the minefield. He tried to relax; slow down his breathing rate, which had imperceptibly quickened. He'd learned from long experience that it was difficult to keep calm if your breathing wasn't under control At the same time, the moment you consciously thought about breathing the rate had a tendency to increase and you would begin to suffer from feelings of slow suffocation. The air would seem to get thinner, causing the lungs to pump wildly and the heart to race. As the symptoms of hyperventilation developed, a trembling feeling would take possession of the limbs and a sensation of giddiness would follow. The odd bodily sensations would be reflected in the brain, inducing a feeling of panic.

Titt took a long, deep breath and let his shoulders drop. With the back of his hand he wiped away a thin film of sweat from his brow as he watched Cheney retrace his steps from the chart table to the centre of the control-room.

'Port ten .... steer 060.' Cheney's voice rang out like a pistol shot.

All eyes swivelled towards him.

Cheney stepped forward a pace, closing the gap between him and the helmsman. The film strip in the gyro repeater started to edge its way across the visor as the vessel answered to her helm. Cheney stood back. He turned to face the asdic cabinet, his features drawn up into a snarling expression.

'Winch?' he snapped. 'Start the M.D.U. Sweep five degrees either side of the ship's head.'

'Steady on 060, sir,' the helmsman reported quietly. 'M.D.U. started, sir. Sweeping five degrees either side of ship's head.'

Cheney gripped the hoist wire of the periscope. 'Very well, Winch,' he nodded. 'Carry on your sweep.'

The ticking of the control-room clock could be heard as the minutes passed. Instinctively, Titt straightened up and . craned his head to look over the crowded control-room towards the asdic cabinet. Winch had the headphones glued to his ears. Alone, of all the men on board, he was the only man who was in contact with the world outside. It was a heavy responsibility but Winch bore it with calm concentration.

Titt could just see the top half of the fifteen-stone, bulky figure jammed into the asdic operator's seat. The face was clearly etched in profile by the light falling on it from the console against the dark background of the cabinet. With a little feeling of surprise Titt noticed for the first time how Jewish he actually looked. He'd never really thought of Winch as a Jew before. It was the sort of thing that hadn't meant anything; neither to Winch or the crew. As far as the fore-ends was concerned he was just another bloke who happened to be the H.S.D. on the boat and that was all. Some of the crew liked him, some of them didn't, but it had nothing to do with his being Jewish. Stanley was about the only one who ever referred to it, offering him a fag and asking him if he didn't mind it not being 'kosher' and that sort of thing. But Winch had never taken offence and seemed to find the idea just about as amusing as the bantam seaman did. But then Stanley baited everybody. There was a coloured bloke back on the parent ship whom he even called Sambo, going through a mime routine of strumming a banjo, and the bloke would just flash his white teeth in a broad grin.

An odd thought crept into Titt's head. Here they were, all on a submarine and perhaps somewhere ahead there was another submarine, only it was called a U-Boat. There would be men on board doing the same kind of job as they were and suffering the same kind of hardships. They would even have an H.S.D. on board (or whatever they called it in the Kriegsmarine) he might even be as good at his job as Winch was, but there was one thing certain – he wouldn't be a Jew.

Titt looked at the senior asdic rating with renewed interest, trying to discover what it was about him that made a Jew so different from anybody else, as some people claimed. Was it something to do with the nose; the dark wiry hair? But then look at the skipper. (He looked at him, studying the face carefully.) The nose might be a bit thinner and the hair straighter than Winch's but that was all. There was no doubt that they both looked like members of the same race or religion, it was only when you came to things like speech and manner that they were as different as chalk and cheese. What was a Jew anyway? Was it a race, or was it a religion? Christ, Titt thought to himself, here's me wearing a Palestine medal on my number one's, spent eighteen months in and out of the place, been to Tel Aviv and Jerusalem and I don't really know whether the Jews are a kind of clan or a religious sect ...

Winch's head twisted fractionally.

'Mine dead ahead, sir.' There was no sign of panic or urgency in the flat Yorkshire tones.

Cheney gripped the periscope hoist wire more tightly, 'Starboard ten,' he said.

The seconds ticked away. 'Another one, sir; dead ahead,'

Cheney bit into his knuckle. 'All right, Winch. Let me know when it's on the port bow.'

The tiny clicking sound of the gyro repeater could be heard as the ship's head paid off. 'On the port bow now, sir.'

Cheney turned to the helmsman. 'Wheel amidships.'

Titt had a quick mental vision of the bulbous, horned, metal spheres that were strung out in front of them. He felt a quick pang of fear as a cold hand seemed to clutch his intestines. His muscles twitched as nerve endings sparked off and sweat began to ooze through the opened pores of his skin. And all the time an alarm system clanged off in his head, telling him to run; to get the hell out of it.

'Contact lost, sir.'

'Very well, Winch. Carry on your sweep.'

Titt felt the tension ease out of his muscles. He took a deep breath, preparing himself for the next contact report, thinking he'd rather be in action any time. And this was only the beginning, there was the whole day to get through. Hours and hours of it yet. Christ, it was worse than the rack.

Jock Bain, on the foreplanes, happened to look round and caught sight of Titt leaning nonchalantly against the watertight door. He wondered what the hell he was grinning at.

In the next hour Winch picked up no fewer than fifteen positive contacts. Almost monotonously he· reported each one and went on calmly with his sweep. The tension in the control-room began to build up as the submarine turned and twisted in her efforts to avoid the mines. Mingled with the heavy smell of diesel oil there arose a new odour, as fear prised open skin pores and activated the sweat glands of the half-crouching men. With the rise in tension there came concurrently a rise in temperature. Air leakage from the high pressure line and the inhalation and exhalation of the same volume of air by the jammed bodies had begun to push the thermometer up. But the change went unnoticed. Like animals feigning death the men had frozen into rigid positions – listening.

The use of the mine-detecting unit for all its advantages only made the crew more uncomfortably aware of the nearness of the deadly explosive bulbs. Most of them would have preferred to run the gauntlet blindly. They had their reasons. The moment you altered course to dodge a mine in front, the stern, swinging round, could collide with one you had previously avoided, in the way that a man walking along a thoroughfare with a long plank on his shoulder could catch someone behind him a blow as he swung round to dodge someone in front. Another serious disadvantage arising from the use of the unit was that the high frequency signals it transmitted could be picked up and plotted by detection devices ashore.

Though the M.D.U. was able to give a physical picture of what was happening it had a severe psychological effect on the members of the crew in the control-room. For the rest of the crew, scattered throughout the boat, it didn't matter, they were cut off anyway and had no way of telling whether they were within a yard or a cable's length of a mine.

Head lowered slightly, Cheney stood by the big periscope clutching the hoist wire as a support. Occasionally he would move from this position to consult the chart. The rest of the time he spent evaluating reports from the asdic cabinet and keeping a hawk-like eye on the compass.

Eleven long minutes had passed since Winch had last reported a mine. Strangely enough, with each sweep of the second-hand of the control-room clock, the men's anxieties, far from being diminished, were increased. There seemed something ominous about such a long gap without anything being reported. It was almost as if a trick were being played on them. A cunning device to soothe their senses and lull them into a false sense of security, then –

'Mine dead ahead, sir.'

Practically the whole of the control-room jumped. 'All right, Winch ... Port ten, helmsman.'

The bows began to swing round in evasive action. 'Mine, red 05, sir ... 04, sir... 03 –'

'Port fifteen ... What is it bearing now, Winch?'

'Now bearing ... green 01.'

'Midships, helmsman. Steady as you go.'

No sooner had the helm been put on when Winch reported again.

'Mine ahead, sir,' and before Cheney could make a

further alteration of course, Winch gave another warning: 'Another one bearing red 05, sir.'

The crew tensed and looked at Cheney at the same time as they made their own split second deductions from the asdic report. It looked as if they were approaching a whole string of mines at the worst possible angle. In this the minefield could be compared to a fence with a number of gaps in it. Approaching it from head on allowed maximum opportunity for success, but the moment the angle of convergence was changed the gaps would correspondingly narrow and the chances of slipping through proportionately lessen.

Cheney released his grip on the hoist wire. His head came up. 'Starboard fifteen.'

The helmsman spun the wheel over madly.

From somewhere for'ard, the tube compartment or the fore-ends, at a guess, a sound was heard. Everyone immediately recognised it as alien. They held their breaths, not daring to move as they listened. A big, unspoken question revolved in their minds – 'What was that?'

Cheney acted instantly.

'Wheel amidships.' There was a low note of urgency in his voice. 'Now steady as you go.'

'Eeeeekk! Eeeeeeeekkk!' The ominous sound grew and filled the control-room. It was as if an enormous door was slowly being dragged open on rust-stiffened hinges.

No one could doubt it any more.

They had picked up a mine wire. And somewhere at the end of the wire there was a mine, with its glass-like horns ready to break off at the slightest touch and allow sea-water to get in and set up a chemical reaction that would spark off its firing circuit. Within a second of that happening they would all be blown clean out of the water.

Mulholland shot up out of his hammock when he heard the noise. He landed on the mess deck in his stockinged feet with a heavy thud. Kennedy spun round as if a grenade had gone off. The Brasso ran out on to the deck from the tin he held in his hand, but he wasn't aware of it. The strange noise and the sight of Mulholland leaping from his hammock had frightened him. His mind filled with fear, he could only dimly associate the two incidents as being connected; but it was in some unfathomable way.

The sound grew louder, jarring the nerves like a dentist's drill. Perturbed and shaken, Kennedy looked round for the T.G.M. Wells had also stopped what he had been doing. He put the tap down quietly and looked at Mulholland. The eyes of the two men were linked in common understanding.

They both knew what the sound implied.

'What is it, Chief?' Kennedy asked in hushed tones.

Wells took a deep breath. 'It's a mine wire, son. It looks as though we've picked up a mine.'

Kennedy shrank back as if he'd been touched by a leper. Then the fear, which he'd been struggling hard to control, gave way to a wave of terror. An enormous sense of claustrophobia gripped him. He wanted to scream; to flee from this water-surrounded, steel dungeon in which he suddenly found himself imprisoned. He felt like a trapped animal.

The sound came again, threatening to tear his nerves to shreds as it seeped through his eardrums and reached down as far as his bowels. His body felt as if it were coming apart. He no longer seemed to be in control of it. It affected him like those awful dreams he'd suffered from, following the death of his father. Momentarily he became disorientated, feeling his presence in the submarine was all a mistake; a joke that had somehow turned ugly and dangerous. In the whirl of his thoughts he found he had an almost irrepressible urge to cry out to the one person who had been closest to him all his life, his mother. But she couldn't help him now. He was on his own. With the shock of a knife being plunged into his stomach it came to him that he might never see her again.

Suddenly he wanted to be sick.

Wells took him by the arm. 'Okay, son,' he said, steering him firmly towards the mess table where Mulholland sat. He knew what the youngster was going through. At all costs he had to prevent him from feeling isolated and alone. For a moment he thought of waking Barbour so that the whole torpedo team would be mustered, but he dismissed the idea.

Barbour was asleep and blissfully unconscious of what was happening. It was better he was left alone; there was nothing he could do anyway. Nothing any of them could do.

He pushed Kennedy down on to the locker bench and sat down himself on the edge of the table. Mulholland sat silently with his arms folded tightly across his chest.

The awful grating sound had stopped.

Wells shot a glance at the sea-pressure gauge on the bulkhead. The needle was creeping round slowly. They were gaining depth slowly but the movement seemed to lack control. It was as if they were just sinking. There was still no sound. Had they got free of the mine wire or had it snagged up somewhere, anchoring itself to the hull?

Wells cocked his ears. He couldn't hear the soft purr of the motors. Had the captain stopped them and was trying to hold a static trim? Or was he allowing the boat to sink slowly downwards. If the mine wire had been caught up on the hull they would be like a rabbit trapped in an explosive snare, not daring to struggle. To move forward could bring the mine down on them like a descending lift. Maybe that was Cheney's plan then, to move downwards not forward, and use the mine's own buoyancy to effect their escape. If they dragged the mine down with them it would have all the more tendency to shoot upwards and perhaps free the wire, in the same way as an empty bottle would if it were held under water. But whatever the captain did now there was no telling what could happen. It was a gamble. Wells loosened the top button of his overall suit. It was becoming unbearably hot, despite what the thermometer said.

'Looks as if we're hooked up,' Mulholland said flatly. Wells ignored the comment and turned to face Kennedy who was sitting upright with grotesque stiffness, his face the colour of chalk.

'Go through the drill of blowing up the tubes,' he said brusquely.

Kennedy's eyes widened and his lips twitched as if he'd lost the power of speech. He couldn't believe he'd heard the T.G.M. right. 'Eh?'

'I said go through the drill of blowing up the tubes. What's the matter with you? Have you got cloth ears?'

Wells rapped.

'The t-t-tubes ...?' Kennedy stammered, looking towards Mulholland as if seeking confirmation that the T.G.M. had suddenly gone mad.

'Never mind him. He can do it in the dark with his eyes shut. It's you I want to hear the drill from. Now, let's have it,' Wells prodded mercilessly.

Kennedy's head wagged bewilderedly. 'But –?'

'Do I have to tell you again? Go through the drill I said,' snarled Wells. 'You might have to do it on your own one day. Now get cracking. Right from the start,' his voice crackled with authority.

Kennedy licked his lips, stole a glance at the impassive Mulholland and hesitatingly began: 'The first thing you do is to crack open the valve –'

Wells interrupted. 'At the order, "Blow up tubes"...'

'Oh? At the order "blow up the tubes" you first crack open the valve from the –'

'No, you bloody well don't.'

Kennedy took a deep breath and sighed despairingly.

'Now start again. What do you check first? The very first thing?'

The young torpedoman bit his lips and concentrated. 'You 'mmmm? Yes, that's right, y-you check that the bow cap doors are closed. Then you –'

'What was that you said?' The T.G.M.'s lips were a tight compressed line. 'Just say that again.'

Kennedy flushed nervously. 'I said that you checked the bow cap doors were –'

'Were what?' Wells asked in an iron voice.

Kennedy realised his mistake. 'Were shut,' he

replied in a guilty whisper.

'That's better … shut! That's the word; don't forget it. I won't tell you again. Never, repeat never, use the word "close" on board a submarine. That's a dirty word to a submariner and if I ever hear you use it again I'll have the skin off your back.'

Kennedy stared miserably at the space between his feet.

'Now, there's a good reason for that,' Wells went on. 'Like everything else in the Navy it has a purpose and its purpose is to prevent misunderstanding. When you have misunderstandings you have accidents and a submarine's no place have accidents. You might get away with an accident on a surface ship but not on a submarine – not very often anyway. So remember, the word is "shut". In our language "close" does not exist, okay? Now start again.'

Kennedy looked crestfallen. He kneaded the skin of his forehead with probing fingers. 'Sorry, Chief.'

'Okay, son. Just remember never to use that word again … Now carry on.'

Racking his brains to get the complicated procedure right, Kennedy began a recital of the drill all over again.

Wells had guessed right. They were in a tight spot. They had picked up a mine wire and dragging along the hull it had snagged up somewhere midships, near the control-room.

The crew heard it scraping along the side of the hull like the approach of a blind man fumbling with a stick – and then it had halted. Cheney immediately stopped both motors. To make further way with the mine wire fouling the hull would have been courting disaster. Without way on the submarine began to sink like an inert whale. Cheney had anticipated this, knowing how impossible it was to achieve a state of absolute negative buoyancy where a submarine could remain suspended at constant depth.

He shot a look at the depth gauge. The bubble had begun to slide aft, indicating they were slightly heavy by the bow, and the big needles on the gauges were quivering nervously. 'Get the angle off,' he snapped at Brangwyn.

Brangwyn, in charge of the trim, reacted quickly. 'After pump, pump from for'ard,' he called out.

The switchboard operator shot his hand out and flicked over the pump indicator switch at the same time as he rang up the pump-station in the after-ends. The light on the pump indicator panel flashed on and was followed a second or two later by a red light that indicated the pump was operating. From somewhere under the deck a low gurgling sound was heard, like a bath emptying, and then there was silence again as the pump stopped.

Cheney stepped over to Brangwyn and muttered a few words in his ear. Brangwyn nodded and unhooked the Tannoy.

'First-Lieutenant here. I want you to listen carefully,' the echoing sounds generally associated with the system were strangely absent, screened off as they were by the heavy water-tight doors. 'It appears that we may have picked up a mine wire ... The captain is trying to keep a static trim. No one is to move from his present position until further orders. Is that clear? Everyone must remain absolutely still.' He flicked off and hung the instrument up.

In the far corner by the exchange Stanley grinned widely. 'I'm glad I wasn't in the middle of a slash,' he remarked. There was a slight titter of nervous laughter from the corner. It stopped abruptly as Cheney wheeled round warningly.

Now all eyes watched the bubble again. It was a difficult and delicate operation, trying to hold a static trim. Like balancing a knitting needle on the edge of a razor blade. A little too much one way or the other and the needle would tilt and slip off its point of fulcrum. They wouldn't have much chance if they plunged down in ninety fathoms of water.

It was an awesome dilemma they found themselves in. Above was a mine. Beneath a cruel tonnage of water that would crush the life out of them as effortlessly as a man crushes an ant with his boot. And for all they knew the shore listening station might have picked up the high frequency signals from the mine detection unit. Perhaps the whole place was about to seethe with anti-submarine forces.

The possibility of detection had occurred to Cheney. He had a talent for seeing all possible exigencies and dealing with them. It was this talent that had kept him, and his crew, alive in the past. It was also the reason he was a highly successful submarine commander.

'Start an asdic sweep, Winch. Stop the M.D.U.'

'Aye, aye, sir.' Winch switched off the unit and readjusted his headphones.

Brangwyn inched closer to the planesman watching the bubble as if it were some strange kind of deadly insect. It had crept back amidships. He prayed that it wouldn't begin to slide forward now as so often happened when you desperately needed a trim. Had he pumped too much water aft? Were they now stern heavy? The bubble seemed to be holding, but for how long? How long could he expect to keep this up without using the planes or the motors? And another thing they were making depth. Not much but slowly and surely like a water-logged hulk.

He half turned to speak over his shoulder to Cheney, never taking his eyes off the bubble for an instant. '105 feet, sir,'

'Yes. I know,' Cheney said, the tone in his voice clearly implying he didn't need to be reminded.

Brangwyn stiffened slightly at the rebuke.

He heard Cheney's voice again asking for an asdic report and automatically he swung to face the cabinet. But Winch had completed his sweep and anticipated the question.

'Full sweep carried out, sir. Nothing to report.'

The control-room itself seemed to breathe a relieved sigh. The needles on the gauges trembled and moved forward again in a clock-wise direction. They were still sinking slowly. Suddenly it dawned on Brangwyn what Cheney was trying to do. He was deliberately pulling the mine down with them. Instead of tugging at its sinker on the sea bed it would be tugging at sea wire which was attached to the hull. Somewhere above it would be struggling like a kite on the end of a line in a high wind.

'Do you think it might work, sir?' he whispered over his shoulder. The question was genuine but it also let Cheney know that the first-lieutenant was alive to his purpose.

161

Cheney grunted an unintelligible reply.

'Watch her,' he suddenly said. 'She's losing the trim.' Brangwyn's eyes flicked over the spirit-levels. The bubbles appeared to be nailed to the centre.

'Pump from aft, man. She's stern heavy,' Cheney urged in warning tones.

Even as Brangwyn gave the order to pump there was a barely perceptible movement from the bubble. The red indicator by the switchboard flashed on as the pump started up and sucked greedily at the water in the trimming tank.

'Stop pumping,' he cried.

The bubble came to a halt just abaft the centre line and began to ease back. He had caught her in time but it had been thanks to Cheney.

They were now at a depth of 115 feet. The mine must be tugging madly at the wire that was holding it back in its efforts to shoot upwards. Would it break free? Brangwyn, like everyone else, strained his ears to note the slightest sound that would indicate the wire parting company with the hull. Everyone was keyed up listening. When the sound came it caught them unawares. Winch's voice hit them like a bombshell.

'H.E. bearing red 80,'

Cheney twisted round. 'What is it, Winch? What does it sound like?'

Winch shook his head negatively. 'Difficult to say, sir. It's a bit mushy, but ... it sounds like diesel.'

'Revs?'

'Can't really tell, sir. Mebbe around 100, or something like that but it's hard to say.'

'Very well, Winch. Keep an eye on her.'

'Oh, God,' Brangwyn thought. 'Just what we need.

A bloody A/S trawler coming out for a snoop around.'
Brangwyn was worried that she might drop a few
patterns of depth charges if she suspected there was a
submarine about. She wouldn't enter the minefield of
course but the effect of compression waves on the trim
would be disastrous.

122 feet.

Winch's voice came from the cabinet. 'Range
appears to be closing, sir. H.E. still a bit mushy. Now
bearing, red ... 82, sir.'

Cheney withdrew the knuckle of his forefinger from
his mouth. 'Very well, Winch. Keep reporting her. Let
me know if you can get a range,'

The minutes dragged past.

For Brangwyn it was becoming more and more
difficult to keep a trim. The bubble looked unstable and
threatened to slip away. Still no sign that the mine wire
had broken free.

Cheney came to a decision. He had to act before
they lost the trim altogether and went in to an
uncontrollable dive. It might free them but to check the
dive he'd have to blow main ballast. Anyone listening
on hydrophones would be bound to hear it. But worst
of all he'd have to cope with the boat behaving like a
wild stallion bang in the middle of a thickly sown
minefield.

'All right, Number One. We'll start the motors. Use
the starboard. Right, let's get moving.'

Brangwyn sucked in his breath and braced himself.
He turned to the stoker manning the telegraphs. In a
voice he tried to keep firm he said: 'Slow ahead
starboard.'

Within seconds a sound was heard like that of a

distant powerhouse generator. A faint pulse rippled through the deck as power was sucked up from the battery cells and transmitted to the screw. Once more the submarine felt alive.

'Starboard ten,' Cheney ordered.

Making way through the water the submarine crept forward gingerly in a circling movement as helm and screw forced her round.

A loud creaking sound filtered through the hull. Like an enormous foot treading on a loose floorboard in an empty house.

Eeeeeeekkk! It sounded again; an ominous scraping sound came to an abrupt halt. Then a series of hammer like blows fell; terrible sounds that made the blood run cold. Bang! Bang! Bang! Another tortured squeal of metal rubbed against metal – and silence.

They were free.

Aircraft Carrier

John Winton
Copyright © John Winton 1980

This was the best time of the day, actually, just before dawn. The Pacific stars were still shining, the flight deck still wet with overnight dew, or perhaps a little spray, misting up from the bows. The island was a large shadow against the stars, all shapes and angles, curious how it was all dark but you could still see the island. It was there all right, with one pale light from a scuttle. Somebody careless with their black-out. There was the sound of waves brushing the ship's side, steadily, on and on, with their own sort of rhythm. No heat yet, no action, no gunfire, no adrenalin, no shouting or tumult.

The pilots had all mounted and settled in their seats. Time to test the radio, try the oxygen. They were all alone in their cockpits, but corporate parts of the squadron. That same smell of oxygen. The aircraft handlers were down there; you could only see their ghostly Lucite wands. Over to port, old Dainty Delilah was flying off her Seafires for the dawn CAP. Lovely aircraft, beautiful and delicate, like a rapier, but no good for this Pacific war. Out here they needed something with a sock in it, the good old F4U Corsair, like a long-range meat-axe. One hundred and twenty switches and gauges, no less. Like a cinema theatre Wurlitzer. A far cry from the old Fairey Fulmar's air speed indicator, fuel gauge and compass. As they used to say, one to get there, one to get back and one for luck. This one was a hydraulic marvel. Spread and folded the wings, lowered and raised the undercarriage and arrester hook, it even cocked the guns for you, did everything but cheer when you hit a Zero.

Check the binoculars on their cord, rest them comfortably on the chest. 'Start up Corsairs!' Waiting for the loudspeaker, it still came as a shock that sent a trembling down to the fingernails. Snap switches on, while the handler takes hold of the prop. He is not even a face yet, not even any geometric figure, but the movement is recognizable. Away goes the- engine and down goes the handler, flat on the deck, sensible fellow, as he has been drilled to do. There was precious little clearance for a man's head between the tip of the prop and the flight deck. Out chocks, with a gesture, release brakes, take up revs, and roll forward. The wands beckon onwards. Lights waved in front, there goes the tail-light of the next ahead. Now this one, now us. Roll forward, fine pitch on the propeller, hear the engine note changing as the propeller feathers. Rolling now, the island a blur to starboard, that pressure on the back and buttocks, up comes the tail and go, across the bows with a zip like a physical sound. Out and across the sea, skimming over an ebony table with tiny purple cups chiselled into it, then changing to pink, and up into the sunlight. Just like that. Brilliant, splintered light flooding the cockpit, making everybody blink and scrabble with one hand for the sun-glasses in the top-pocket.

A shape glided into the corner of one eye, up and to the right. It was Ronnie, the starboard wing man.

'Orange Two, this is Orange Leader, closer and lower.' That was their call-sign, Orange. Was it a fruit or was it a colour? Yesterday it was admirals, last week it was carpets and cabbages. Tomorrow it would be dances or animals or party games.

'Orange Two, roger, Skipper.'

A steady roaring in the ears, the fighter direction officer was on the fighter net. 'Orange Leader, this is Miss Britannia, Orange Leader, this is Miss Britannia …' Stanley audibly had not had his breakfast yet. 'Course to steer to target, confirm two-nine-one. Time to target seventy-nine minutes, seven and nine, seventy-nine.'

'This is Orange Leader, roger.' He sounded like a bloody tombola caller.

Turning to port and looking down, *there* was a sight to take the breath away. Sunlight was just touching the masts and funnels of the task force, and throwing the shadows of the ships over the shining sea. That almost rhymed. Twenty-five clear-cut geometrical designs emerging from a dark sea. They were steaming into wind and Corsairs were peeling off one by one from Madame Fifi, our chummy ship. That was probably Robert Weston and his merry men.

'Dodgers nine o'clock!'

That would be the CAP. Seafires they were, four of them, in what the war correspondents, in their own inimitable way, called a 'cap of steel'. These were high above the task force and there were two more at sea level, flying to and fro. That was the 'Jack' patrol. That

167

was where you put the new boys, or the old boys who had lost their bottle. Back and forward, back and forward, at sea level; it was enough to drive you round the bend.

The four carriers, with their Avenger TBRs still ranged aft, were like pale autumn leaves from this height, oblong shapes, tablets of grey steel on the water, with dots moving off their surfaces. That one, second in from the west, was Miss Britannia. That was home. There was the briefing room, the wardroom, the bar, the cabin, the bunk, down there.

'Orange Leader, this is Miss Britannia. Hot Line says nobody at the party.'

'This is Orange Leader, roger.' That was the report from the two early-morning reconnaissance Hellcats. Nobody at the party. No Japanese aircraft on the runways. But nobody at the party did not mean nobody at home.

'Orange Section, this is Orange Leader, down now and flat arse!'

Down they went, lower and lower, a hundred feet, fifty, twenty, lower and lower until you could feel your sphincter squeezing up, well below the radar beams, three hundred knots flat-arsing over the sea. One hesitation, a slip of the finger, at this height and this speed, and goodbye Dolly we must leave you. But you could trim the elevator tabs, and fly to keep the nose down. Lift your hand and the Corsair would lift upwards.

'Orange Two, this is Orange Leader. Lower.' Ronnie hated low flying. He always tried to cheat.

The sea skimming towards you had a mesmeric effect, it took all the feeling out of your legs, so that only the part of you showing in the cockpit really existed.

Twenty-five minutes to target time. Very interesting people, the Japanese. They were dirty fighters and one dreaded to be shot down. There were already grim rumours in the fleet about what had happened to the boys chopped down over the oil refineries in Sumatra in January. No hard fact, but the air intelligence staff buzz was that they had been taken to Singapore and executed. Johnnie was one of them, almost the best wingman Skipper had ever had. He made one pass too many over one of those jungle airstrips. Skipper could see it now: a raw scar of red mud in a brilliant green, with a muddy river just beside it. Hard to think of Johnnie ending up in a Japanese execution cell. Yet the Japanese had more than forty different words for different kinds of winds, gales, breeze, zephyrs, call them what you like. *Hatakaze*, wind that causes the flapping of a flag. *Siokaze*, wind that springs up at the turning of the tide. *Nadakaze*, wind over the open sea. They called their destroyers after them. *Tatikaze*, wind caused by the stroke of a sword. *That* was more like it. *Kamikaze*, divine wind. They had used those over the Philippines and were using them now over Okinawa.

The sea was still flashing along below.

'Orange Section, this is Orange Leader, *feet up!*' It was time to go up and take a look.

At ten thousand feet the islands came up at first as no more than darker patches of the blue ocean, already in sunlight. As we in dreams behold the Hebrides. Theirs was the middle one, Ishigaki, the one shaped like a boot, or a saucepan, or a bloodstain. They had dozens

169

of different words for islands, too. Out binoculars, already focused and adjusted correctly, to save seconds. Hold it, there *was* something on that runway. It was difficult to tell in the haze but it looked like a bomber. Probably wheeled out of a cave into the sunlight after Hot Line had pushed off.

The best way in to the airstrip was from the south. But they did that yesterday. Today they would come in from the east, with the rising sun, and how very appropriate. There was a bright-red corrugated iron roof in the middle of the town. They called it the Bus Station. They would go down to sea level again, feet above the water, and flat-arse it into town. Go from specks out at sea to shapes overhead in seconds.

'Orange Section, this is Orange Leader. Down now, and flat out, *break!*'

They wheeled and dropped, down through successive coloured layers of the sky. It was a different world down here, a different existence, with the eardrums constantly swelling and popping.

The island was a low wrinkle on the horizon, and there was something, or somebody, missing.

'Orange Two, this is Orange Leader, get lower. And closer. Ronnie, you *must* fly lower.'

Ronnie was scared. But low in this game meant low, but *low*.

No Hendon Air Display tactics here. High, wide and handsome meant high, wide and dead before dusk.

'Orange Two, still not low enough.' He would have to get rid of Ronnie. 'For Christ's *sake*, Ronnie.'

There were gunpits between the town and airstrip, and the lad dies in them were normally quite good. They would have had their breakfasts by now, and they would be waiting. There was the red roof of the Bus Station, and what looked like a baby's pram in the street, and a bang like a distant shot-gun. Faces in the gunpits looking upwards, and barrels like shiny circles, and some smoke. Now level for the runway. It was made of crushed coral, flushed pink in the sun, with some pustules in it where the Avengers had bombed it and the Japanese had filled in the holes overnight. And so it went on.

And there she was – a fine, fat juicy Betty, perched on the end of the strip. Some figures stood beside it. Some senior Japanese officer on his way from Formosa to Okinawa, or possibly even to Japan. They should have got off at first light. Too late now, *mate.*

They started firing a long way off, the three of them fleeing across the coral. Skipper had harmonized his guns at the butts so that the bullet streams from each wing converged at four hundred yards' range. He armed all the squadron with his own special ammunition cocktail of six ball to one tracer and one armour-piercing. He was satisfied to see, at four hundred yards, the Betty seeming to change shape, as though looked at through a heatwave. The wings fluttered and tore, score marks showed on the fuselage, the figures disappeared from the runway. There were more gunpits at the end, ugly holes like blackheads in an old man's cheek. They lifted up, so close that they almost carried away the Betty's radio aerial, lifted away and up, with that tremendous pressure on the backside, and heads lolling, looking to starboard. There was a whiff of smoke back by the Bus Station.

'Orange Two, this is Orange Leader come in.' There *had* only been three of them on that strafing run. That stupid bugger Ronnie had got himself lost. 'Come in, Orange Two.'

'He's gone, Skipper, he's gone!' A thread of hysteria in Geoffrey's voice.

'Orange Section, form on me.' Must keep the voice-calm. 'This is Orange Leader, what happened? Steady now, just tell me.'

'Over the town, Skipper. Gun got him. Straight through the windscreen. Blew his head off, must have done.'

'This is Orange Leader, roger. Angels thirty, full boost. Go. Course to steer …' A look down at the pad on the knee. 'Zero-nine-zero, magnetic. Nine-oh, as far as we go.'

So, a few feet had made all the difference. A cautionary tale. If it had not been Ronnie, whom one knew, it would have been as funny, in a sick sort of way, as Struwelpeter. This is the tale of Ronnie Bell, who tried very hard, but not very well. No more singing in the showers.

As he climbed, Skipper could see and hear Green and Purple Sections making their runs. The gunners were really alert. Smoke was rolling all over the airstrip. One Corsair went the wrong way, and the other three, like clumsy mallards tumbling in the sky, separated slightly, by what could be a crucial amount. They always were a messy lot. Now that those gunners were in such good practice, something would have to be done about them. Perhaps a simultaneous strafe from ninety degrees to port or starboard, to keep their heads down, while the runway party passed overhead. *Something* would have to be done, anyway.

'Orange Leader, this is Miss Britannia. Make your

cockerel cro-o-o-ow!' Stanley always accentuated that word, drawing it out realistically.

'This is Orange Leader, roger. Orange Section, check IFF.'

The fleet was always in a highly nervous state and anybody, but *anybody*, flying in from the direction of the islands was suspect. All those itchy trigger-fingers fired first and asked later. The fleet's aircraft identification was generally shocking. The Seafire boys, who operated nearer the fleet, had already lost two, chopped down by the fleet's gunfire, dropped by their own mates. With IFF switched on, your special blip, you hoped, would literally clear you on the radar screens.

At 30,000 feet, propellers in coarse pitch, water injection in those long-striding engines, they passed over the Avengers, with fighter cover above and below them, on their way to bomb the runways. Below them, a smudge, just a trace on the sea, was the American air-sea rescue submarine.

Halfway back, they met the veterinary cruiser with its destroyer escort. Every aircraft returning from the islands had to be vetted, by flying once round and close to the cruiser picket, called the veterinary station. It was uncomfortable, and hair prickling, to fly low and slow and steady round a warship and see all her guns trained and following.

'Orange Leader, this is Salem Witch ...' It was the Vet calling. 'Why only three?'

'Salem Witch, this is Orange Leader, Orange Two, George Baker Yoke.' It made him sound like a bandleader.

George Baker Yoke. GBY. Short for Great Blue

Yonder. A somewhat macabre joke, but effective. The initials meant missing, believed killed. The Fleet Air Arm was a mass of initials. They had initials the way other people had complexes and neuroses. CAP. Combat Air Patrol. TBR. Torpedo-Bomber-Reconnaissance. IFF. Interrogatory – Friend or Foe? RAS. Replenishment at Sea. RPC. Request the Pleasure of your Company. WMP. With Much Pleasure. MRU. Much Regret Unable. US. Unserviceable. LMF. Lack of Moral Fibre ...

'Orange Leader, this is Salem Witch, you're clear.' Passed, with flying colours. 'Course to steer, zero-six-six.'

'This is Orange Leader, roger.' Sixty-six. Clickety-click.

As they flew, Skipper kept on missing Ronnie from the corner of his eye. It was like having a limb amputated, like a great gap with a draught pouring in from the cold. Young Geoffrey could move over and take his place. But even when he had swung over to starboard and ranged up alongside, so that Skipper could see his wing-tip rising and falling, feet from his own, Skipper still felt uneasy.

Nearer the fleet, there were more identification screens, invisible veils dropped down to protect the ships from intruders. There were high CAP staring down from above, and low CAP craning their heads to look up, and Jack patrols at three levels, and there were all those radar screens turning and peering and noticing. If your face didn't fit, there were the gunners. Every ship had extra 20 and 40mm guns in every available clear space.

But there was something reassuring about it all.

The bees were returning to a friendly hive. The stings were sheathed, the guards were turning their backs.

'Orange Leader, this is Miss Britannia, have you now visual. Check fuel.'

The returning RAMRODS were stringing into line astern and forming up on their own carriers. Skipper flew down Miss Britannia's port side, working over his check list. Back hood. Full flaps. Down undercarriage, down hook, fine pitch ... There should be a mnemonic for it. Flaps ... Under ... Carriage ... FUC ... Perhaps not.

With a fully worked-up squadron, as they were, they should be able to land on at 22-second intervals. So here they go. He could see Tiny the batsman and the glowing yellow bats he was holding out. Tiny was a big man and he had needed two burly naval airmen to hold him upright when he batted on a returning strike in a rising gale off the Norwegian coast nine months before. The bats looked like undersized oranges in Tiny's enormous fists.

Corsairs had such long engine cowlings that one had to bank to port, turning fairly sharply all the way, to look over the side, and straighten up at the last moment. It should be good. Skipper saw Tiny nodding and knew it was good. White and grey wake from the ship, a smear of brown funnel haze floating away to starboard, the grey-green deck just coming into sight.

Cut, and Tiny whipped away his bats and jack-knifed as though somebody had just punched him in the stomach. Each deck landing was the same as all the others, and all the others were totally different from each other. Skipper cut the throttle, and there was a thump and a drawing back. Open the throttle again, hook clear, signals from ahead, roll forward, select wing hydraulic folding lever, down comes the safety barrier, the great bulk of the island shuts out the sun to starboard. Skipper was aware of seeing the next astern land on, in his mirror. Rolling forward, wings almost meet overhead with a heavy vibration. The marshaller cuts his own throat with an expressive gesture, shut throttles, almost silence. One more RAMROD and one less.

Chief Air Rigger Petre was standing beside the starboard wing trailing edge. Normally he would have come up on the step with some comment, but not this time. He already knew about Ronnie. The flight-deck grapevine was working. For most of the ship the news about Ronnie Bell would not be noticed any more than the slap and bump of a wave against the bows. But in his squadron, for those who had known Ronnie, his death was a space, a hole which had not yet even begun to harden and seal around the edges. Ronnie was dead, so long live everybody else. Besides, it had happened so many times before.

Before he did anything else, Skipper went up to the bridge to see the Captain. It was the first step demanded in a ritual for the dead, the first rung in a kind of hierarchy of commiseration. The Captain was sitting in his huge, high bridge chair, smoking the inevitable dark cheroot, wearing khaki tunic and shorts and a rather comic baseball cap, with a long green peak, which somebody had given him on a visit to an American carrier in Ulithi lagoon. Skipper had never quite fathomed the Captain's real feelings when a member of the aircrew was lost. So much depended upon circumstances. In training, he was critical, concerned, even censorious. In action, he was sympathetic – but that was too uncomplicated a word. The Captain held an unusual emotional balance, taking the loss personally, but looking beyond at its effect upon the whole ship's company.

The Captain's war, like that of all his contemporaries, went back to September 1939, and he had been at sea almost the whole time. In a sense his war had begun even earlier; he had been First Lieutenant of a destroyer in the Mediterranean during the Spanish Civil War, and he had once been a junior officer in an aircraft carrier on the China Station in the early Thirties – an era of junks, pirates, gun-runners and drug smugglers. The Captain was regular, straight-stripe Navy, all Dartmouth, Greenwich and Whale Island. He was, of course, not a flyer and Skipper sometimes suspected he still secretly looked upon flying as vaguely ungentlemanly, unseemly. It was unsporting to hit a man beyond normal gun range. Yet Skipper knew that the Captain recognized his aircrew were now his main armament and that his squadron COs controlled that armament. The Captain would quickly ask his COs' advice, in a way which constantly flattered them. Skipper had come to admire and respect the Captain increasingly as their months of service together had lengthened, and he sometimes felt the Captain's reciprocal interest in himself.

The Captain turned his head at the sound of Skipper's footsteps and, hoisting himself round in his chair, he offered his hand in a curiously formal handshake.

'I'm sorry to hear it, Skipper,' the Captain used the nickname unselfconsciously, as though unaware it could have been his own.

'The same thing?' The Captain knew of the problems they had had with Ronnie.

'Yes, sir. Low but not low enough. If you get right down, you're safer. It is always hard to hit a pheasant going right for your hat. Same principle, sir.'

The Captain nodded at the example, drawn for his benefit.

'He was basically a good pilot, sir, but he would not be taught beyond a certain point.' Skipper shrugged his shoulders. What more was there to say? He had not liked Ronnie much, but then, it was not his business to like or dislike people. His job was to make people fly against the Japanese.

'What exactly happened?'

'I'm not sure, sir, exactly. He was behind me. Geoffrey Tilling, the port wing man, had a better view.'

'Fetch him.'

Geoffrey, when he arrived on the bridge – anxious at the summons, somewhat overawed and awkward with his words – had not much more to contribute than his first description over the R/T as they climbed away from Ishigaki. Ronnie Bell had lifted up for a fatal half-second and the gunners had got him through his windscreen. As he listened to Geoffrey tell his story, Skipper saw what an impossible task the boy had been set: to describe how a colleague had died beside you. The finest poets in the language had faltered at that, and Geoffrey was just a grown-up schoolboy. His father was a water board official and they lived in south London – Croydon or Penge or somewhere. And here he was, explaining to professional naval officers how one of their number had been chopped down in the course of their profession. Because Ronnie had been RN, the only RN officer in the squadron. The rest, including Skipper himself, were all RNVRs. And now there were none. It could be – Skipper hesitated before formulating the thought, even to himself – that Ronnie had died just because he was RN. He had just that shade, Skipper thought, of unbendingness, that tinge of superiority. Off the Sakishima Gunto only the flexible man who was right on top of his reflexes, the real nervous learning reacting man, ever survived.

After the Captain, Skipper went to see Commander (Air) and his assistant, Lieutenant-Commander (Flying), continuing his round of commiseration in order of decreasing seniority. Wings and LittleF, as they were always known, were in Flyco, the small open space with a parapet overlooking the flight deck, where the eternal wind burnished the cheeks and tugged everlastingly at clothing and hair, and would, sooner or later, whisk anything loose away into space. In hurried phrases, whilst the other two craned over to look at the flight deck, answered telephone calls and broadcast messages, he told them what had happened. He minced no words. It was all Ronnie's own fault. *De mortuis nil nisi bonum* was all very well, but here, while the struggle for Okinawa was going on to the north, the living outweighed the dead a million times over. Postmortems might save more lives. So, always the question to be answered was, was it anything wrong in our routine? Was it just Ronnie's own hamfistedness, or is there anything we should be doing to safeguard the rest?

After Flyco, it was Stanley the Fighter Direction Officer, sitting naked to the waist with the sweat running down his chest, in his hot, dark little hell-hole full of radar screens in the centre of the island. Forced draught fans were roaring full bore, and two portable desk fans were trained on Stanley's face, but his office was still as airless and oppressive as an oven. Again the questions, was it the direction, was anything not clear, did we run you into a pig's ear, could he not *hear*? No, said Skipper, no and no and no. It was like visiting and reassuring the relatives of the deceased, in a left-handed sort of way. No, he died a good death. Nothing in his life became him like the leaving of it.

Skipper was always careful about debriefing. It was important not to let it become perfunctory. It was important to listen with attention while the pilots described their experience. One could learn a great deal, about the target, the sortie and the man, from a phrase, from a word, even from a tone of voice. Ops marked the position of Skipper's Betty on his chart of Ishigaki runway, and put a cross for Ronnie on the perimeter where they had flown in. There were, Skipper could see, one or two crosses now beginning to accumulate around that airstrip.

After debriefing, Skipper could have gone to his cabin aft, but the ship was still at Action Stations, State Two, a relaxed state but the watertight doors were shut, as they would be all day, and it would take him a quarter of an hour to get aft. The effort would exhaust him, in the heat. There was a row of cabins in the island, and Skipper was once again amazed to see officers washing and shaving. Was it *really* only a quarter to seven in the morning? For the aircrew, time was disjointed. There was operational time, Japanese gunners' time, and there was ship's time, breakfast time, and there was a personal time, no time for thought. There was a galley in the island and Skipper had breakfast, scrambled powdered egg and fried potatoes which were not potatoes but something called Pom, and tea which tasted of bird-seed. So, it had to be the ready-room, where the chairs were deeper and more comfortable than any others on board. People were going to and fro, brushing irritatingly past Skipper's feet. He wanted to roar at them. Don't you *understand*? he wanted to bellow at them. Can't you see?

There were a thousand things, as squadron CO, he could and should be doing – seeing the Chief Air Tiff about mods to the aircraft and the state of serviceability in general, seeing Michael the Senior P about a replacement in the short term for Ronnie, seeing the squadron Chief about the sailors going up for the next Captain's requestmen and defaulters, seeing Geoffrey about switching to starboard wingman for the rest of today; all these people to see, things to be doing. But Skipper was too tired to do any of them, and dozed off in his chair until Ops shook him for briefing.

Skipper got to his feet. This was a Fleet Air Arm pilot's life – sleep until somebody shook you awake and told you it was time to fly again. Sleep, shake, wake, fly, then sleep, shake, wake and fly.

It was 8.30 and this time it was high CAP for an Avenger bomber strike on Ishigaki. The strike was to be accompanied by another Corsair fighter RAMROD offensive sweep: and the Hellcats from the flagship would beat up Miyako. Skipper was relieved to see that A-Able, his regular Corsair, was available again. He abhorred superstition and strenuously discouraged it in his squadron. A boy could mentally work himself into a physical spin, literally, merely because he flew without his lucky pyjamas on, or his girl friend's teddy bear, or his lucky Australian shilling in his pocket, or his lucky sun-glasses, or his lucky scarf. Ronnie had had a lucky Ovaltinie badge, which he always pinned to his shirt on a strike, and a fat lot of good it had done him. All the same, Skipper could not repress a sense of pleasure and relief in climbing into the familiar cockpit with its hundred familiar scrapes and scuffs and scratch-marks.

High CAP, at an average of 30,000 feet, was an eye-swivelling, neck-wrenching, head-craning business, never flying at the same height or on the same course for more than half a minute, snaking and switchbacking and weaving from side to side and up and down, watching and turning, turning and watching, over the tubby Avengers below. The strike was like a battle far off and long ago, minute bomb bursts on the runways, several separate dust hazes; it was like watching somebody bomb Mars, although Skipper fancied he could actually hear the detonations.

On the way back, Stanley vectored them out to a bogey to the north and Skipper peeled his flight off the top to look. It turned out to be a Liberator not transmitting her IFF properly. It was probably one of MacArthur's, so nobody in the Navy would have been told anything about it. MacArthur and Nimitz were supposed not to get on too well together. They broke off at a mile, but the Liberator had her guns trained on them, so they had not been asleep in that ship.

When they got back they found that the Avengers had lost one, and Dainty Delilah, next in line to port, had lost a Seafire from the CAP. Madame Fifi had a Corsair down from the RAMROD. With Ronnie from the dawn sorties, this was the worst morning so far for the task force off the Sakishima Gunto. This was how it was going to be, not a sudden dramatic rush of losses, as at the Sumatran oil refineries, but a slow bleeding away of the squadrons, day by day. A war of attrition. This was trench warfare in the air, a steady, relentless chipping away at the enemy's strength.

Somebody said that the Corsair pilot was seen to get out and somebody else said the US lifeguard submarine had got him. But the Avenger was a certain goner. It had been seen to plunge into the middle of the main runway on Ishigaki and nobody ever got out. It was the turn of Henry Darling, the Avenger squadron CO, to make the rounds of the Captain, Flyco, the air direction office, and so on. Skipper had barely known the pilot and the observer. Odd that one could serve in the same ship with someone for nearly a year, ever since the strikes off Norway, and hardly know him. In fact, Skipper had known the observer since the days of the big Malta convoy of 1942, but knew nothing about him. But the telegraphist-air gunner, Petty Officer Bennett, had been one of the ship's characters. He was a brilliant deck-hockey player, and much in demand with his accordion 'squeeze-box' at ship's concert parties. So 'Wiggy' Bennett was gone. It was best to forget him, shut him out of your mind.

Later they heard the flagship had lost a Hellcat, ditched into the sea. Somebody saw the pilot get into his dinghy. At the next briefing, Ops mentioned the ditching drill. He had not done that for days, but now it was news again. Otherwise, it was the mixture as before, interpreted in the figures and letters chalked on the ready-room board: weather, call-signs, target photographs, map of gun positions. Skipper felt he could have drawn that from memory.

'What about strays?' he asked. 'Last time, we dosed a Liberator all ready to go.'

'We're looking into that.' Ops' brow wrinkled at the implied criticism.

'That's all very well. Looked at from *here*.' Skipper had not meant the remark to be funny, but everybody else laughed nervously. Ops' brow creased even deeper. He, too, was RN. Score two this morning.

'As I said, Skipper, we're looking into it.'

Skipper sensed the relief on the faces behind him when they heard the target was Miyako, generally supposed to be the less deadly of the two major islands, although Skipper himself could not understand how this opinion had ever grown up. It was six of one and half a dozen whangers on the other. There were already as many crosses on Miyako, perhaps because aircrews eased up slightly there, believing it was a less dangerous target. They should bear down all the harder instead.

Skipper made that point with some force at the squadron 'huddle' – so called after they had all seen that movie about American footballers, and indeed Skipper sometimes felt like a football coach, giving his team a pep talk before they went out on to the field. This was to be an all-out strike, with all the squadron aircraft that were serviceable, eleven of them that morning. Michael, the Senior Pilot, was to take his flight to Karimata, in the northern tip of the island, where the Japanese had a seaplane base, rarely used.

Although Skipper knew what Michael was, and how potentially dangerous such a man could be, he still almost loved him. He probably loved him more for his weakness. Michael appealed to that 5 per cent aberration that *Esquire* magazine said lurked in every man, but was normally no more important or significant than his nipples. But Michael's sympathy, his intuition, his courage, made up for everything. He had a DSC, won over the *Tirpitz* a year before, and the squadron vowed it should have been a VC. Michael was so good a pilot that Skipper told new hands to the squadron to stand up in the goofers and watch him land on. They were lucky to have him. He should by rights have got a squadron of his own by now. Perhaps he would, when this squadron stood down from operations – whenever that would be. Doctors and psychologists who would have wet themselves if they ever went near Ishigaki gave solemn lectures about fear and wounds and resolution in combat and recovery rates and time after operations and nightmares, when the proper solution was staring them in the face: give all air crews a set time on board and have them relieved promptly when their time was up, as the Americans had learned to do, the hard way. As it was, the air group joined and served on, and on, and on, and on, until they dropped – literally.

Miyako was certainly a more pleasant-looking island, greener, flatter and somehow friendlier. It had the same pan-handle shape from the air, a blob and a spit, and it was supposed to have more people on it than Ishigaki. Skipper had once tried to find out about the people of the Ryukyus. The islands had been under Japanese control and closed to all outsiders for years before the war, so the information in the great pile of books and documents from US military intelligence that the Schoolie produced was many years out of date, as their authors admitted. Skipper had started to read them but their dry pedagogic tone defeated him.

Those were people down there, not insects or rock plants. They had babies, they ran from aircraft, they were not even Japanese. There was one old man who knelt in a little walled garden at the edge of the Nobara airstrip, just by the coast. Skipper had passed only ten feet above him on two previous strikes and he had never even looked up. God knows what grew in his little garden – worms, probably. Miyako Shima was in the Miyako Retto, which was part of the Sakishima Gunto, which in turn formed part of Ryukyu Retto, an important chain in the Nansei Shoto. The Japanese had as many names for collections of islands as the Eskimos had for snow. But in the meantime, they were all targets.

There was nothing at Nobara, not even the old man in his garden. It was as bare as a baby's bottom. The runway was swept clean and clear, as though they had come to inspect it. Not a gun spoke, not a funeral note. They turned across the island and headed for Hirara, flying across a neat, delicate and somehow fragile landscape of tiny fields and thin white tracks, spidery links threading between patches of green, with dots of huts. It was a miniature landscape, seen through a diminishing glass.

There was a bit of a harbour on the western coast, nothing much, just a jetty and a couple of wooden fishing vessels. Some Fireflies from Dainty Delilah were busy above it, working it over with rockets and cannon fire. That squadron was full of Royal Marines, all as daft as a blind Chinaman's brush. Their aircraft were rising and falling over the target like starlings. They had probably got hold of a small coaster, not more than fifty tons, carrying fish, or rice, or a bit of coal or some firewood, something very basic, bound to be.

There were some suspicious-looking lumps at the end of Hirara strip.

'Domino, Domino, this is Domino Leader, one run only. Get close. *Break!*' Ronnie's place had been taken by Edward, the squadron spare prick, because Skipper had not wanted to break up any of the other flights. He must be good enough, because Skipper had barely noticed him.

The landscape leaped up to meet them and rocked several degrees before they straightened up on their strafing run. Still no gunfire. And there she was! A great big shiny new Betty bomber again, painted bright blue, large as life and twice as natural. It must be Tojo's birthday!

'Domino, Domino, this is Domino Leader, blood for supper!' It was uncannily like Ishigaki a few hours before, although the light was better, the picture harder and sharper. They fled down the runway on their single pass, firing from a long way off. The Betty was sagging on one wing as they streaked over it.

The guns began as they reached the perimeter and started to climb. With mild surprise, Skipper decided they must have moved the batteries. The angle was new. Somebody once said that gunfire had a smell especially when it hit you. Skipper smelt it now, it was that close. Very much closer than usual. The Corsair shook and began to vibrate as though it wanted to shake itself out of the sky. After near-misses the whole frame seemed to go on trembling for minutes afterwards, as though the cab was as scared as you were. Skipper could feel the unhealthy vibrations through his finger-tips.

'Domino Leader ...' Geoffrey and Edward were both trying to speak at once. Edward fell silent, as the new boy. 'Skipper, I think you're hit, Skipper!'

'Where?'

'Tail-plane.'

'Anything else?'

'Negative.'

,'No smoke?'

'Negative.'

'What's it look like?'

'Fairly bad, Skipper. Like somebody bit a big chunk out.'

'*Big* chunk?'

'Well ... maybe ... *fairly* big ...'

'Roger. This is Domino Leader, we'll go straight back. Course one-one-five magnetic.'

When Skipper tried to steepen his climb, the Corsair gave an ominous lurch and the vibration nearly wrenched the joystick out of his hands. Skipper's mouth flooded with saliva and his stomach knotted until he gasped with pain. With horror he realized that his bowels had almost betrayed him. He knew now what the Americans meant when they said 'keep a tight arsehole'. He remembered the lad in the early days at Quonset Point who had demonstrated conclusively that a Corsair would not pull out of a spin. The boy had obviously known what was going to happen to him before he hit, and had lost control of his bowels. That cockpit afterwards, as somebody said, was like an abattoir, with blood and shit. Skipper's fingers and palms were slippery with sweat and he could feel the goose-pimples all over his legs. He had a fleeting sensation of disgust, as though he were sitting in a bath of slime. He swallowed the saliva and tried to relax his forehead muscles, which had contracted the skin in a fierce scowl. At least the gauges were all steady and reading correctly. It was just this vibration which went and then came again, as though the Corsair had suddenly remembered it was hurt.

Stanley, who never missed a trick, passed the bearing and distance of the American lifeguard submarine, in case Skipper needed her, and reassured Skipper that the air-sea rescue Walrus amphibian was being spotted on deck for use. He had also cleared Skipper's flight with the veterinary cruiser, which passed them without comment. Why, thought Skipper, if they can do that in an emergency, why can't they do it all the time, without all this tedious spotting and delays?

Miss Britannia, when they reached her, was already steaming into wind as hard as she could go. Skipper could see that from her broad, boiling, creamy wake. He also caught the green light, meaning they were ready. On his final circuit, Skipper made his checks. *Alles in Ordnung* ... Flaps, undercarriage, hook ... Hook ... That was it ... No hook. Obviously shot away. As he turned on his finals and approached the deck, Skipper gritted his teeth and winced. It was *going* to be all right. He *would* not follow Ronnie Bell so soon. The vibration was much more serious, so that it seemed that only Skipper's grip was preventing the Corsair falling apart. Skipper made up his mind, he would *not* follow Ronnie Bell. There was Tiny, there was the deck, and there was an almighty bang as he crossed the round-down. After the cut, the aircraft seemed to stop flying and literally fall out of the sky. The undercarriage held and the aircraft began to roll, seeming to accelerate rather than slow down. One by one, the impotent arrester wires slipped underneath and the big barrier was rushing up at appalling speed. In a dreamy moment Skipper remembered that old song, 'And loud in my ears, the sweet angel choir *sang* . . . "Floating in, floating in, float, float, float, barrier *prang!*"'

The grinding and rending of the wires, biting into the Corsair's wings and engine cowling, seemed to go on for a surprising time. When it stopped, Skipper stayed in his cockpit, still resting his weight against his straps. Cracking show, I'm alive! But I've still got to render my A25! He could tell, by the unnatural angle of the aircraft, that something was very wrong back aft. Chief Air Rigger Petre's face appeared to starboard, with one of the helmeted crash-men in the whitish-grey fearnaught suits. Skipper undid his straps and stood up, turning round to look aft. The tail-plane was gone, completely. Two aircraft handlers, far aft on the flight deck, were manhandling its distorted shape towards the ship's side. The end of Skipper's Corsair was just a jagged-edged hollow tube. Skipper felt his mouth swimming with saliva again and, remembering just in time to turn to port away from Chief Air Rigger Petre, he bent over and vomited down the side of his aircraft. When that stopped, Skipper found, to his shame and dismay, that he was crying.

THE
PROS╈ATE
CANCER CHARITY

All of the profits made from sales of *A Seaman's Anthology of Sea Stories* will be donated to The Prostate Cancer Charity.

Founded in 1996, The Prostate Cancer Charity is now the UK's leading charity working with people affected by prostate cancer. We fund research, provide support and information and we campaign to improve the lives of men with prostate cancer.

We encourage, support and fund research into the causes, prevention and treatment of prostate cancer. The long term aim of our research is to save lives and improve life for men with prostate cancer. Since 1994 we have invested over £7 million.

Our Helpline is the only UK-wide prostate cancer Helpline staffed by prostate cancer specialist nurses. Our nurses offer free and confidential information and support to anyone affected by prostate cancer. Our online message boards also provide a platform for people affected by prostate cancer to share experiences and support. All information we send out is free and tailored to the needs of men with prostate cancer and their families. Our publications are evidence based, independently reviewed and award winning.

See page 195 for how to contact us

What is the prostate gland?

Only men have a prostate gland. The prostate is usually the shape and size of a walnut. It lies underneath the bladder and surrounds the tube (urethra) that men

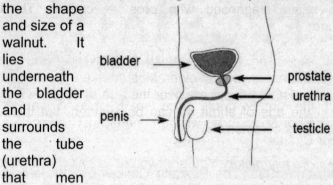

bladder

penis

prostate

urethra

testicle

pass urine and semen through. The prostate gland's main job is to make most of the fluid that carries sperm, called semen.

The prostate gland can get bigger with age and may press on the urethra, causing problems with passing urine.

What is prostate cancer?

Normally the growth of all cells is carefully controlled in the body. As cells die, they are replaced in an orderly fashion. When cancer develops, the cells start to multiply in an uncontrolled way.

If this happens in the prostate gland, prostate cancer can develop. In most cases this is a slow growing cancer and it may stay undiagnosed because it never causes any symptoms or problems. However, this is not true for all men. Sometimes prostate cancer cells can grow quickly and move outside the prostate. They may then cause symptoms in other parts of the body, such as the bones.

What are the risk factors?

There are several factors that increase the chance of a man being diagnosed with prostate cancer. These include:

- *Age* The risk of getting prostate cancer gets higher as you get older. Most men diagnosed with prostate cancer are over the age of 50. Men from the age of about 40 can be affected, but this is less common.

- *Family history* You are two and a half times more likely to get prostate cancer if your father or brother has been diagnosed. The risk increases more if your relative was under the age of 60 when they were diagnosed, or if more than one relative has been diagnosed with prostate cancer.

- *Ethnicity* African Caribbean men are three times more likely to be diagnosed with prostate cancer than white men. Researchers are looking at what may be the cause of this increased risk, but diet and genes probably play an important part.

- *Diet* The typical Western diet is high in saturated animal fats and red meat. Researchers think this may be responsible for the higher rates of prostate cancer seen in Western countries. By reducing the amount of animal fat in your diet and eating more of certain fruits and vegetables, you can improve your overall health and may lower your risk of prostate cancer developing or spreading. Read our page on <u>diet</u> and prostate cancer for more information.

What changes should I look out for?

The main types of prostate problem are:

- a non-cancerous enlargement of the prostate called Benign Prostatic Hyperplasia (BPH) – this is the most common prostate problem
- inflammation or infection of the prostate (prostatitis)
- prostate cancer
- Each of these prostate problems can cause similar symptoms. These may include:
- A weak or reduced urine flow

Needing to urinate more often, especially at night

- A feeling that your bladder has not emptied properly
- Difficulty starting to pass urine
- Dribbling urine
- Needing to rush to the toilet – you may occasionally leak urine before you get there

Less common symptoms include:

- Pain when passing urine
- Pain when ejaculating
- Pain in the testicles

In the UK:
Prostate Cancer is the most common cancer in men
35,000 men are diagnosed with prostate cancer every year
One man dies of prostate cancer every hour

www.prostate-cancer.org.uk
Confidential Helpline: 0800 0748383

Monday to Friday 10am - 4pm, plus late night Wednesday 7pm - 9pm
Calls are free of charge from UK landlines. Mobile phone charges may vary.
Calls may be monitored for training purposes. Confidentiality is maintained between callers and The Prostate Cancer Charity.